POP
for SUPERHEROES
PSYCHOLOGY

DOES THIS CAPE MAKE ME LOOK FAT?

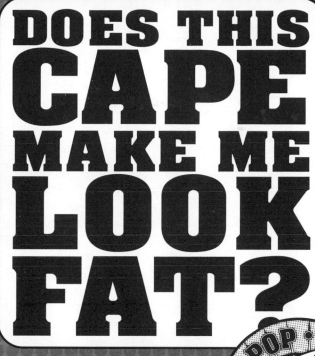

POP SUPERHEROES for PSYCHOLOGY

CHRONICLE BOOKS

SAN FRANCISCO

BY CHELSEA CAIN & MARC MOHAN
ILLUSTRATIONS BY LIA MITERNIQUE

ACKNOWLEDGMENTS

THANKS TO EXCALIBUR BOOKS & COMICS, OUR EDITOR
STEVE MOCKUS, EVERYONE AT THE JOY HARRIS AGENCY,
JASON KAGEL FOR INTRODUCING CHELSEA TO COMICS
THAT SUMMER IN NORTH CAROLINA, BETH KRAUSE FOR
DRIVING MARC TO THE COMIC BOOK STORE ALL THOSE
YEARS, AND, OF COURSE, THANKS TO LIA FOR HER
MARVELOUS ILLUSTRATIONS, DESIGN RAZZMATAZZ,
AND FOR ALWAYS BEING SUCH A GOOD SPORT.

LIBRARY OF CONGRESS CATALOGING-IN-PUBLICATION DATA AVAILABLE.
ISBN-10: 0-8118-5200-8
ISBN-13: 978-0-8118-5200-5

PRINTED IN CANADA

DESIGNED BY LIA MITERNIQUE

DISTRIBUTED IN CANADA BY RAINCOAST BOOKS
9050 SHAUGHNESSY STREET
VANCOUVER, BRITISH COLUMBIA V6P 6E5

10 9 8 7 6 5 4 3 2 1

CHRONICLE BOOKS LLC
85 SECOND STREET
SAN FRANCISCO, CALIFORNIA 94105
WWW.CHRONICLEBOOKS.COM

FOR
ELIZA FANTASTIC MOHAN
WHO WILL ONE DAY
GET TO READ HER
DADDY'S COMICS.
BUT NOT UNTIL
SHE'S SIXTEEN.

CONTENTS

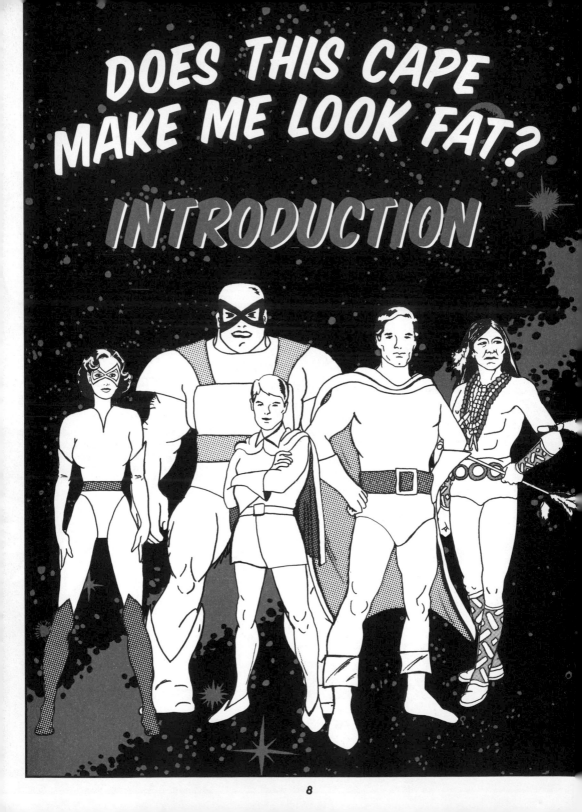

In many ways, the life of a **superhero** is **fantastically exciting**: the intergalactic battles, the **opportunities for travel**, the cape. But beyond the obvious challenges of the superhero lifestyle (No way! The alien sentinels are invading **AGAIN**?), there are many more tests of **inner strength**. After all, who's looking out for your emotional needs, while you're busy **saving the world**? Before you can be a superhero to Metropolis, Gotham, or Cedar Rapids, you must first be a **superhero to yourself**.

If you are reading this book, then you have already confronted the biggest hurdle on the path to self-actualization: **admitting to yourself that you need help**. Perhaps your teammates held an intervention. Perhaps an errant duplication ray created an exact copy of you, with the opposite personality, and you were stunned to discover that your friends liked the **copy** more than they liked **you**. Whatever your reasons for **exploring your reality**, we welcome your effort and encourage you to **embrace the emotional renaissance** that is now at your gloved fingertips.

CHAPTER #1

WHAT'S IN A NAME?
WHAT YOUR MONIKER SAYS ABOUT YOU

LET'S FACE IT: WE ALL MAKE ASSUMPTIONS ABOUT PEOPLE BASED ON **THEIR NAMES**. SOMETIMES THESE ASSUMPTIONS TURN OUT TO BE **SHAMEFULLY OFF THE MARK**. BUT THAT FIRST IMPRESSION CAN PROVE LASTING. SUFFICE IT TO SAY THAT IT'S IMPORTANT TO UNDERSTAND WHAT **SIGNALS** YOUR NAME MAY BE SENDING.

EVERYBODY HATES ME

The name *The Grim Avenger* or *Dark Apocalypse* may have sounded thrilling when you first chose it, but others who hear it may assume that you are a bad guy. Feeling socially ostracized? Perhaps this is why.

HOW TO TELL IF YOUR NAME IS INTIMIDATING

It has a scary word in it (e.g., Massacre, Fang, Napalm).

People flee when you approach.

You keep getting mail from an evil organization trying to recruit you.

You have trouble making friends.

WHAT TO DO ABOUT IT

Adopt an alias.

Hire a publicist to promote your good works (see page 134).

Consider wearing a costume without an image of a skull on the chest.

Preface all public interaction with the phrase "I am not here to kill you."

Smile (unless doing so activates your death ray).

Conversely, you may find that the public and your peers do not take you very seriously. For a superhero, that can prove to be a real career barrier.

EVERYBODY THINKS I'M A JOKE

PIXIE LAD! ER, WHERE'S CAPTAIN STEEL?!

HOW TO TELL IF YOUR NAME IS TOO LIGHTWEIGHT

IT HAS A **SILLY-SEEMING WORD** IN IT (E.G., SPARKLE, DAISY, RAINBOW).

IT ENDS WITH **BOY, GIRL, LAD, LASS, OR MITE,** OR IS PREFIXED BY **LITTLE, L'IL, WEE, OR TINY.**

IT'S THE NAME OF AN **ADORABLE BABY ANIMAL** ("FAWN," "CUB").

THE LAST FOUR LETTERS ARE **"ETTE."**

CAN I CHANGE MY NAME?

CHANGING YOUR NAME IS **ACCEPTABLE**, ESPECIALLY IF YOU ARE IN A TRANSITION PERIOD—SAY, MOVING FROM A **SIDEKICK ROLE TO A TEAM ROLE**. AVOID CHANGING YOUR NAME TOO MANY TIMES, HOWEVER, AS IT CAN BECOME **CONFUSING** AND COULD CREATE THE IMPRESSION THAT YOU ARE **INDECISIVE** AND, WORSE YET, **BAD AT CHOOSING NAMES**. NOTE THAT MULTIPLE NAME CHANGES MAY ALSO COMPLICATE YOUR MAIL DELIVERY.

CHOOSING A NEW NAME

Avoid umlauts.

In most cases it is advisable to limit yourself to two words or six syllables.

Be sure to avoid unintentionally embarrassing abbreviations that might end up on your chest emblem. (We can all learn from the cautionary tale of the Astonishing Silver Sprinter.)

Alliterations are always popular and are easy to remember.

There are two approaches to choosing a name.

#1

CHOOSE ONE THAT IS EVOCATIVE OF YOUR POWERS.

#2

CHOOSE ONE THAT COMMUNICATES NO SPECIFICS BUT NONETHELESS INVOKES AWE IN THOSE WHO HEAR IT. (ADJECTIVES SUCH AS MARVELOUS, FANTASTIC, AMAZING, ETC., ARE A GOOD PLACE TO START)

Suffering from low self-esteem? Consider the second approach. You'll be amazed at how much more confident you feel when your friends and family have to refer to you as **"Lady Spectacular."**

EXAMPLES:

GOOD NAME		BAD NAME
MR. FABULOUS	⇨	MR. KOWALSKY
METAL MAN	⇨	TIN BOY
SGT. STRONG	⇨	SGT. STEROID
OCEAN GIRL	⇨	GUPPIE
LADY LUCK	⇨	THE CHEATER
DR. BRAIN	⇨	SMARTY PANTS
LIGHTSPEED	⇨	THE WHIZZER
BEAR BEAST	⇨	KOALA LAD

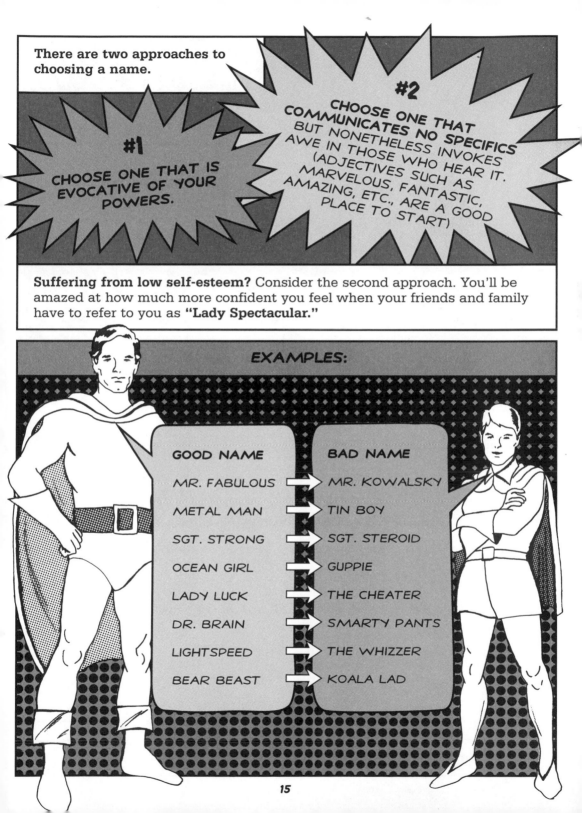

CHAPTER #2

GETTING ALONG WITH YOUR SIDEKICK

THE SIDEKICK RELATIONSHIP CAN BE PARTICULARLY **DICEY**, AS IT IS, BY DEFINITION, **INEQUITABLE**. THIS MAY LEAD TO RESENTMENT ON THE PART OF YOUR "**LESSER HALF**." DO YOU FIND THAT YOUR SIDEKICK IS NOT AS WILLING TO THROW HIS BODY IN FRONT OF A **SPEEDING LIGHT SPEAR** AS HE USED TO BE? NO ONE WANTS A SIDEKICK WHO SULKS ALL THE TIME OR **REFUSES TO WAX THE INVISIBLE JET**. IF YOU SENSE THAT YOUR RELATIONSHIP MAY BE **SOURING**, TRY SOME OF THE FOLLOWING **MANAGEMENT TACTICS**.

STRATEGIES FOR IMPROVING THE HERO/SIDEKICK RELATIONSHIP

GIVE POSITIVE FEEDBACK; PRAISE IMPROVEMENT.*

MAKE HIM FEEL VALUED.

LISTEN TO HIS CONCERNS. CONSIDER INSTALLING A SUGGESTION BOX AT HQ.

INCREASE HIS RESPONSIBILITIES.

AVOID DIRECT ORDERS. INSTEAD, PHRASE DIRECTIVES IN THE FORM OF A SUGGESTION, SUCH AS, **"YOU MIGHT CONSIDER ..."**

CONDUCT ANNUAL PERFORMANCE REVIEWS. [SEE SAMPLE]

TRY TO SEE THINGS FROM HIS POINT OF VIEW.

LET HIM DRIVE (SOMETIMES).

YOU MIGHT CONSIDER NOT LEAVING YOUR BOOSTER PACK WHERE I CAN TRIP OVER IT.

YOU MIGHT CONSIDER MODULATING THE TONE OF YOUR BATTLE CRY.

* Be careful of telepaths — they can tell when you're being insincere.

ANNUAL SIDEKICK PERFORMANCE REVIEW
RATE YOUR SIDEKICK ON A SCALE OF 1 TO 7, WITH 1 BEING
"FAR BELOW EXPECTATIONS" AND 7 BEING "GREATLY EXCEEDS EXPECTATIONS."

GENERAL

1 2 3 4 5 6 7   INTEGRITY
1 2 3 4 5 6 7   WILLINGNESS TO SERVE
1 2 3 4 5 6 7   ABILITY TO WORK WELL WITH OTHERS
1 2 3 4 5 6 7   COMMITMENT TO DEFEATING EVIL
1 2 3 4 5 6 7   CREATIVE PROBLEM SOLVING IN DANGEROUS ENVIRONMENTS
1 2 3 4 5 6 7   ACCEPTANCE OF RESPONSIBILITY FOR DISASTROUS OUTCOMES

APPEARANCE/ATTITUDE

1 2 3 4 5 6 7   HYGIENE
1 2 3 4 5 6 7   PUNCTUALITY
1 2 3 4 5 6 7   CONGENIALITY
1 2 3 4 5 6 7   BRAVERY

SKILLS AND ABILITIES

1 2 3 4 5 6 7   JUDO   1 2 3 4 5 6 7   ANIMAL TRAINING
1 2 3 4 5 6 7   KARATE   1 2 3 4 5 6 7   NOT GETTING CAPTURED
1 2 3 4 5 6 7   JUJITSU   1 2 3 4 5 6 7   COSTUME DESIGN
1 2 3 4 5 6 7   JUGGLING   1 2 3 4 5 6 7   ANSWERING FAN MAIL
1 2 3 4 5 6 7   BALLET   1 2 3 4 5 6 7   GYMNASTICS
1 2 3 4 5 6 7   PILOTING   1 2 3 4 5 6 7   COMPUTER PROGRAMMING
1 2 3 4 5 6 7   COOKING   1 2 3 4 5 6 7   INTERGALACTIC LANGUAGES
1 2 3 4 5 6 7   CLIMBING   1 2 3 4 5 6 7   ROBOTICS
1 2 3 4 5 6 7   ASTRONOMY   1 2 3 4 5 6 7   VEHICLE MAINTENANCE

AREAS FOR IMPROVEMENT

MISSIONS COMPLETED WITH PARTICULAR ACCOMPLISHMENT (PLEASE LIST)

OTHER COMMENTS

If it becomes clear that your relationship cannot be salvaged, encourage your sidekick to join an all-sidekick crime-fighting team. It might be just the kind of supportive environment that your little buddy needs. Drop by his new HQ just to say hi, but not so often that he feels that you're checking up on him.

WHAT TO DO IF YOUR SIDEKICK DIES

DON'T PANIC.

Replace him as soon as possible with someone else who fits in the costume. A close physical resemblance to the previous sidekick will help avoid awkward questions.

SIDEKICK #1

SIDEKICK #2

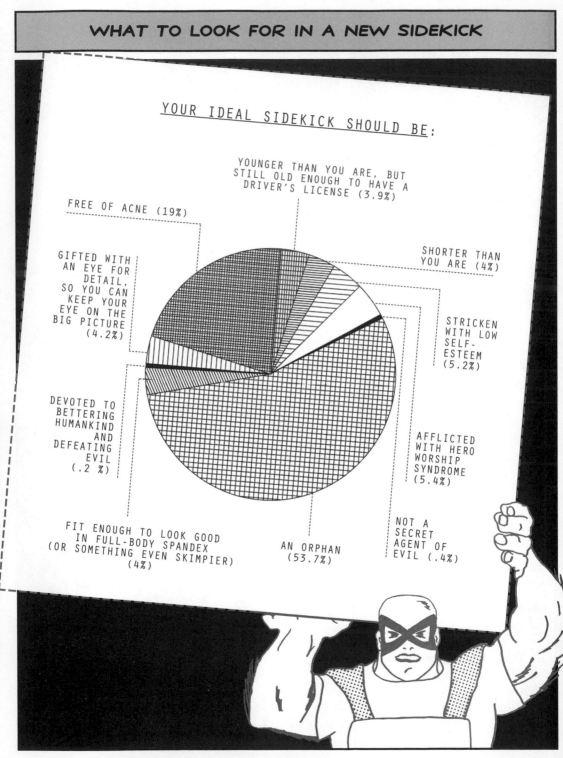

YOUR IDEAL SIDEKICK SHOULD BE:

YOUNGER THAN YOU ARE, BUT STILL OLD ENOUGH TO HAVE A DRIVER'S LICENSE (3.9%)

FREE OF ACNE (19%)

GIFTED WITH AN EYE FOR DETAIL, SO YOU CAN KEEP YOUR EYE ON THE BIG PICTURE (4.2%)

SHORTER THAN YOU ARE (4%)

STRICKEN WITH LOW SELF-ESTEEM (5.2%)

DEVOTED TO BETTERING HUMANKIND AND DEFEATING EVIL (.2 %)

AFFLICTED WITH HERO WORSHIP SYNDROME (5.4%)

FIT ENOUGH TO LOOK GOOD IN FULL-BODY SPANDEX (OR SOMETHING EVEN SKIMPIER) (4%)

AN ORPHAN (53.7%)

NOT A SECRET AGENT OF EVIL (.4%)

WHEN YOUR SIDEKICK IS A PET

A MONKEY

PETS CAN MAKE VERY GOOD SIDEKICKS, ALTHOUGH SOME ARE BETTER THAN OTHERS.*

CONSIDER:

A DOG

A HAWK

A FALCON

A HORSE

AN ALIEN DRAGON

* The ideal animal sidekick should have a neck that you can tie a cape around.

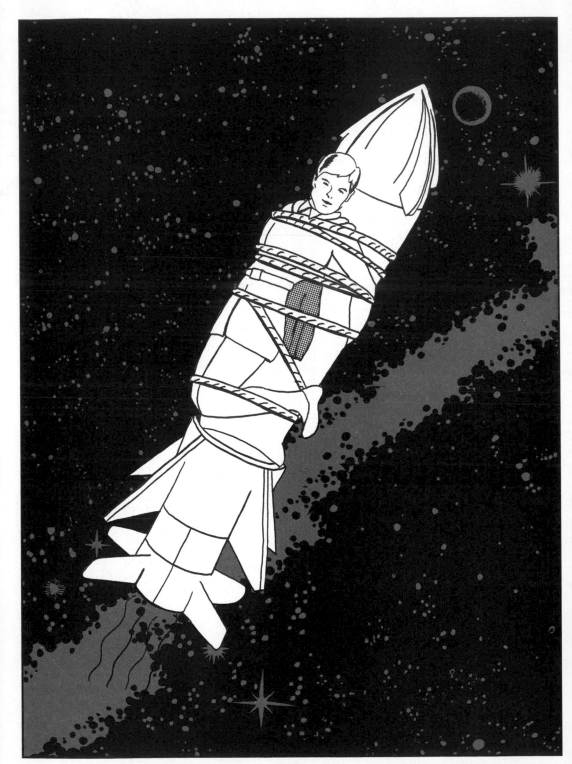

CHAPTER

#3

ADVICE FOR SIDEKICKS

YOU TOOK THE GIG THINKING IT MIGHT LAST A YEAR. NOW, FIVE YEARS LATER, YOU'RE STILL WORKING AS A SIDEKICK. ONCE DISMISSED AS THE **INTERNSHIP OF THE SUPERHERO INDUSTRY**, SIDEKICKING HAS EVOLVED INTO AN **ACCEPTED CAREER PATH** FOR MANY STRUGGLING YOUNG SUPERHEROES LOOKING TO BREAK INTO THE BIG TIME. HANG IN THERE. IF YOU CAN ENDURE THE CATCALLS, RIBBING, AND HOUSEHOLD CHORES INHERENT TO THE SIDEKICK ROLE, IT CAN LEAD TO **SUPER OPPORTUNITIES**.

THE FIVE HABITS OF HIGHLY EFFECTIVE SIDEKICKS:

1. REPRESS YOUR INNER "WARD."

2. DON'T PLAY THE VICTIM.

3. PRACTICE LOYALTY AND FIDELITY.

4. KNOW WHEN TO LEAVE THE NEST.

5. COME UP WITH A GOOD CATCHPHRASE.

AVOIDING THE "WARD" LABEL

One of the most common mistakes sidekicks make is getting branded as a "ward." Take precautions to avoid this at all costs.

☐ DON'T LIVE WITH YOUR ALPHA HERO.

☐ RETAIN YOUR OWN CHECKING ACCOUNT.

☐ DO NOT ALLOW YOURSELF TO BE ADOPTED.

☐ MAKE AND MAINTAIN FRIENDS OF YOUR OWN.

☐ DON'T ALLOW YOURSELF TO BE REFERRED TO AS "JUNIOR" OR "KID."

☐ DO NOT WEAR COSTUME HAND-ME-DOWNS.

☐ DO NOT ALLOW YOURSELF TO BE ENROLLED IN A PREP SCHOOL.

☐ AVOID WORKING FOR A WEALTHY SINGLE BACHELOR.

NOTE: If you are already a ward, get a financial commitment in writing.

AVOIDING PLAYING THE VICTIM

ARE YOU ALWAYS GETTING YOURSELF CAPTURED? IF YOU ARE FEELING IGNORED BY YOUR ALPHA HERO, YOU MAY BE SUBCONSCIOUSLY PUTTING YOURSELF IN HARM'S WAY IN AN EFFORT TO ATTRACT HIS ATTENTION. HAVE YOU RECENTLY FOUND YOURSELF IN THREE OR MORE OF THE FOLLOWING SCENARIOS?

TRAPPED IN A BELL JAR IN THE BASEMENT OF A SPOOKY HOUSE

MANACLED SPREAD-EAGLED IN A VILLAIN'S LAIR

STRANDED ON A DOOMED PLANET

BLASTED INTO ANOTHER DIMENSION

TIED TO A CHAIR

HELD HOSTAGE IN AN UNDERGROUND MAGMA CAVERN

TRAPPED IN ANOTHER BODY

SHRUNKEN AND HERMETICALLY SEALED IN A JAR

PARALYZED IN A STASIS FIELD

FROZEN IN ICE (OR ICE CREAM)

LOCKED UP IN A SECRET GOVERNMENT TESTING FACILITY

STRAPPED TO A ROCKET

HOGTIED AND HUNG OVER A POOL OF SHARKS

TIED TO RAILROAD TRACKS

TEETERING ON THE EDGE OF AN ACTIVE VOLCANO

BURIED ALIVE

BOUND AND GAGGED ON TOP OF A TALL BUILDING

BEAMED TO A DISTANT GALAXY

REGRESSED TO A PRIOR EVOLUTIONARY STATE

BANISHED TO THE PAST OR FUTURE

ENGAGING IN THIS SORT OF RISKY BEHAVIOR MAY HAVE SERIOUS CONSEQUENCES. NEXT TIME YOU'RE FEELING NEEDY, CONSIDER SIMPLY ASKING FOR A HUG.

AVOIDING A BAD REPUTATION

The upward social striving and serial monogamy of some sidekicks has led to the public impression that sidekicks can play fast and loose with their loyalty. Many alpha heroes are skittish about taking on a sidekick only to have her split after an enormous investment of time and training. (This has led to the rise in popularity of three-year contracts with nondisclosure agreements.) Certainly it can be attractive to "hook up" with a new hero, especially after several years of service that may have become boring and familiar. But if you can weather the tough times, a long-term relationship can prove very rewarding.

KNOWING WHEN TO LEAVE THE NEST

Some sidekicks want to strike out on their own before they're really ready. That is not advisable. Instead consider forming an all-sidekick group. Such groups can offer some independence while still providing an emotional "comfort zone" and the support of like-minded young people.

SIDEKICK PERSONALITY DISORDER

There is evidence to suggest that some sidekicks suffer from so-called sidekick personality disorder. Sidekicks with Sidekick Personality Disorder (SPD) may find that they remain sidekicks for their entire working lives. Sidekicks with SPD should *not* form an all-sidekick group, as very little would ever get done.

DO I HAVE
SIDEKICK PERSONALITY DISORDER?

T F   I HAVE TROUBLE GIVING ORDERS.

T F   I LIKE BEING CALLED "KID."

T F   I DON'T LIKE LIVING ALONE.

T F   I FEEL LOST WITHOUT THE
        GLOVED FIST OF AUTHORITY.

T F   I EMBRACE DANGER YET SHY
        AWAY FROM PUBLIC RECOGNITION.

T F   I HAVE 35 PAIRS OF LITTLE
        ANKLE BOOTS.

COMING UP WITH A GOOD CATCHPHRASE

It's important to remember that catchphrases are within the purview of the sidekick, whereas battle cries are reserved for the alpha hero. So as not to step on anyone's toes, you will want to keep your exclamations limited to pre- and postfight banter and let your alpha hero do the mid-confrontation hollering.

CREATING CATCHPHRASES

IT'S EASY! JUST USE ONE OF THESE TRIED-AND-TRUE FORMULAS:

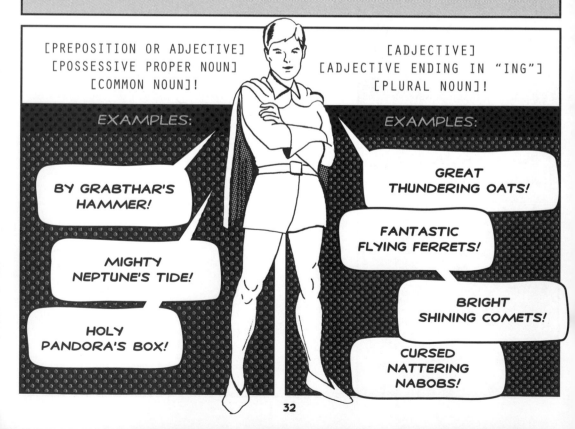

[PREPOSITION OR ADJECTIVE]
[POSSESSIVE PROPER NOUN]
[COMMON NOUN]!

EXAMPLES:

BY GRABTHAR'S HAMMER!

MIGHTY NEPTUNE'S TIDE!

HOLY PANDORA'S BOX!

[ADJECTIVE]
[ADJECTIVE ENDING IN "ING"]
[PLURAL NOUN]!

EXAMPLES:

GREAT THUNDERING OATS!

FANTASTIC FLYING FERRETS!

BRIGHT SHINING COMETS!

CURSED NATTERING NABOBS!

CREATING BATTLE CRIES

IT'S [FILL IN THE BLANK] TIME!

EXAMPLES:

IT'S TUSSLIN' TIME!

IT'S REGRETTING-YOUR-EVIL-ACTIONS TIME!

IT'S SCUFFLIN' TIME!

OR SIMPLY:

ARGHHHHH!

OTHER SUPERHERO EMPLOYEES WHO MAY HAVE CATCHPHRASES:

RECEPTIONISTS
BUTLERS
CHAUFFEURS
PILOTS
LAB ASSISTANTS
LAWYERS
HANDYMEN
NANNIES
ROBOTS
HOUSEKEEPERS
IT SUPPORT PERSONNEL
NURSES*

* Nurses are often taken hostage by villains. This can prove emotionally draining for the hero, who always has to come to the rescue. It is advisable to avoid hiring/dating nurses if possible.

CHAPTER #4

GETTING ALONG WITH YOUR PARTNER

AN EQUAL PARTNERSHIP REQUIRES THE **ONGOING COMMITMENT** AND **SENSITIVITY** OF BOTH PARTIES. KEEP THE LINES OF COMMUNICATION OPEN AND FIND WAYS TO MAKE YOUR PARTNER **FEEL SPECIAL**. A SUCCESSFUL PARTNERSHIP SHOULD PLAY UP THE **STRENGTHS AND POTENTIAL** OF BOTH HEROES AND LEAVE EACH FEELING FULFILLED AND PRODUCTIVE. OF COURSE, **COMPLEMENTARY NAMES AND COSTUMES** ARE KEY.

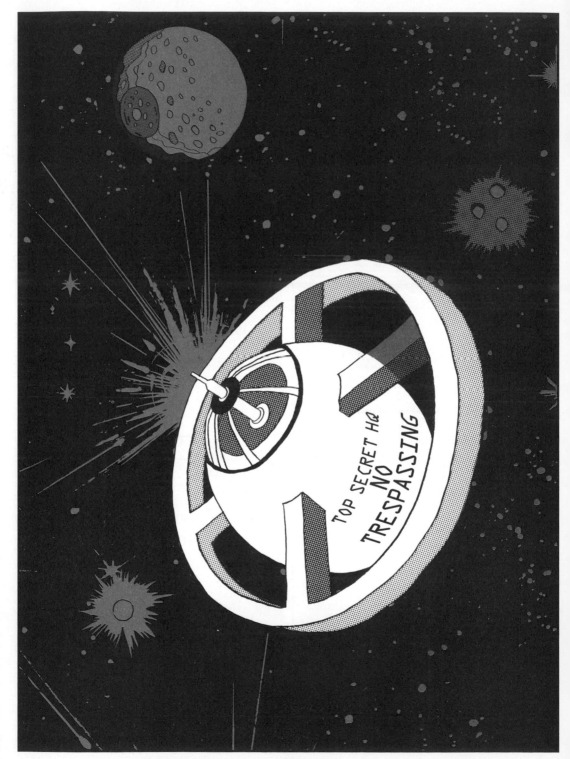

CHAPTER #5

YOUR EMOTIONAL SANCTUARY

YOU PROBABLY SPEND A FAIR AMOUNT OF TIME AT YOUR **HQ**. THE NEXT TIME YOU'RE THERE, **TAKE A LOOK AROUND.** WHERE IS IT SITUATED? IS IT IN A **LARGE CITY**? IS IT ON AN **ICEBERG**? IS IT IN A **DISCLOSED LOCATION** OR A **TOP-SECRET** ONE? IT'S IMPORTANT TO CREATE A SPACE WHERE **YOU FEEL SAFE**, BUT IT IS ALSO IMPORTANT TO CONSIDER WHAT KIND OF MESSAGE YOUR HQ IS SENDING.

TYPICAL UNDISCLOSED HQ LOCATIONS

CAVES

FORTRESSES

EXTRADIMENSIONAL REALMS

THE MOON

CUSTOMIZED RECREATIONAL VEHICLES

ISLANDS

SPACE STATIONS*

BASEMENTS OF UNASSUMING HOMES

SECRET CITIES

*IN GEOSYNCHRONOUS ORBIT.

TYPICAL PUBLIC HQ LOCATIONS

MANSIONS

BROWNSTONES

SKYSCRAPERS

FLYING CITADELS

If your HQ is super top secret, you may be sending the following signals:

You are a loner.

You are not always in complete control of your powers and therefore need to isolate yourself to protect others.

You are so weak, you don't dare expose yourself.

You conduct dangerous experiments, possibly involving antimatter.

You are not in the best of favor with the government.

The public doesn't approve of you.

IF YOUR HQ DOESN'T INSPIRE YOU, CONSIDER INVITING AN EXPERT IN TO REDECORATE.

However, a disclosed HQ location poses some other challenges:

Constant enemy attacks
Property taxes
Stalkers
Junk mail

```
   WHEN I AM IN MY HQ
     I FEEL LIKE:

(A) BATTLING EVIL A LITTLE.

(B) BATTLING EVIL A LOT.

(C) BECOMING EVIL.

(D) INVITING PEOPLE OVER TO
    PLAY TENNIS AND HANG OUT
    BY THE POOL.

A: GOOD, B: BETTER, C: BAD, D: BEST
```

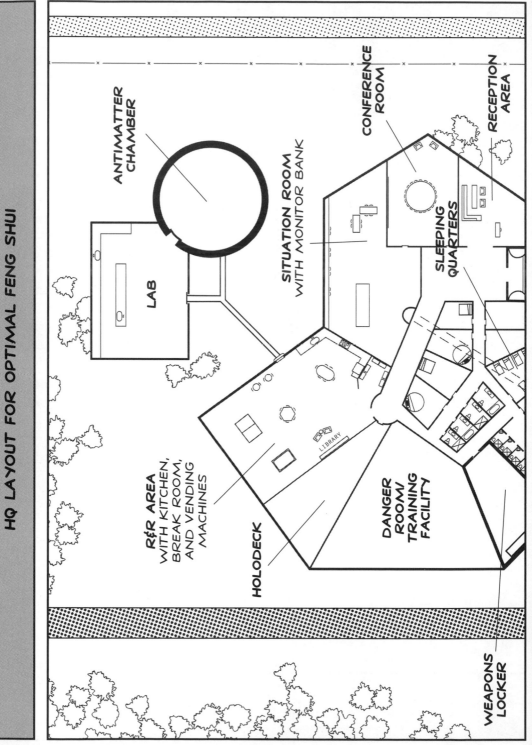

HQ LAYOUT FOR OPTIMAL FENG SHUI

ANTIMATTER CHAMBER

LAB

SITUATION ROOM
WITH MONITOR BANK

CONFERENCE ROOM

SLEEPING QUARTERS

RECEPTION AREA

R&R AREA
WITH KITCHEN, BREAK ROOM, AND VENDING MACHINES

LIBRARY

HOLODECK

DANGER ROOM/ TRAINING FACILITY

WEAPONS LOCKER

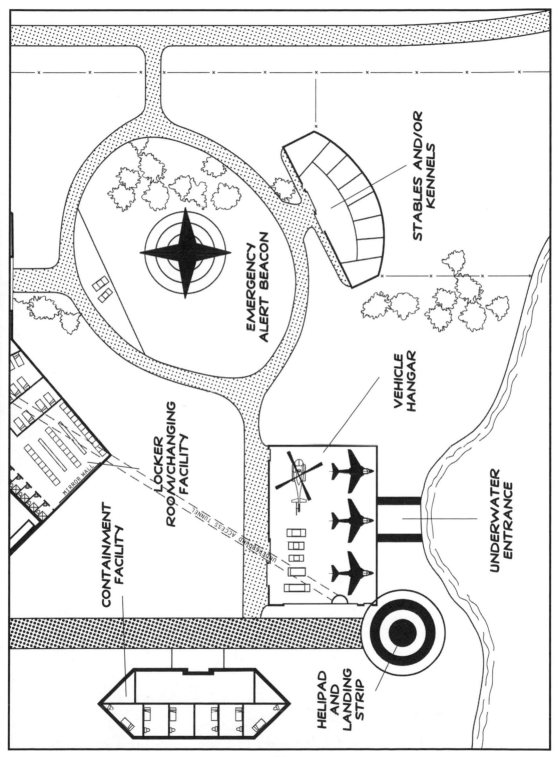

STABLES AND/OR KENNELS

EMERGENCY ALERT BEACON

VEHICLE HANGAR

UNDERWATER ENTRANCE

LOCKER ROOM/CHANGING FACILITY

MIRROR WALL

UNDERGROUND ACCESS TUNNEL

CONTAINMENT FACILITY

HELIPAD AND LANDING STRIP

CHAPTER 6

THRIVING IN A TEAM ENVIRONMENT

MANY SUPERHEROES CHOOSE TO WORK AS PART OF A **TEAM.** SOME ENJOY **THE COMPANY, THE STRENGTH OF NUMBERS,** AND **THE PRESTIGE.** OTHERS ARE JUST LOOKING FOR A **WAY TO KEEP THE BILLS DOWN BY SHARING EXPENSES.** WHATEVER YOUR REASONS FOR JOINING, YOU'LL FIND THAT A TEAM ENVIRONMENT POSES SOME PARTICULARLY CHALLENGING **PSYCHOLOGICAL DILEMMAS.** LET'S LOOK AT THEM NOW.

HOW TO ATTAIN GREATER INFLUENCE AND RESPECT AMONG YOUR TEAM MEMBERS

SPEAK UP.*

ATTEND ALL MEETINGS.**

BE PUNCTUAL.***

VOLUNTEER FOR UNGLAMOROUS ASSIGNMENTS LIKE MONITOR DUTY OR ESCORTING PRISONERS THROUGH DIMENSIONAL PORTALS.

SEEK OUT OPPORTUNITIES TO SHINE—BUT NO SHOWBOATING.

HELP CLEAN UP AROUND HQ.****

EMBRACE PROFESSIONAL DEVELOPMENT OPPORTUNITIES, SUCH AS JUDO TRAINING IN THE DANGER ROOM OR COMMUNICATION TECHNIQUES.

* Unless, of course, your voice is actually a hypersonic weapon, in which case write your suggestion on a Post-it or sear it into the wall with your heat vision.

** You never know when the secret and only way to penetrate your nemesis's harder-than-steel exoskeleton will be revealed.

*** Just because your colleague *can* travel through time doesn't mean he *likes* doing it just to suit your schedule.

**** Again, you may think that your teammate's super-speed makes her the ideal candidate for dish duty, but remember, she could be having super-fast fun, too.

DON'T STEAL YOUR TEAMMATES' GIRLFRIENDS.

DON'T COPY THEIR COSTUMES.

DON'T MAKE FUN OF OTHER PEOPLE'S POWERS.

GET A PH.D. IN SOMETHING SCIENCEY.

47

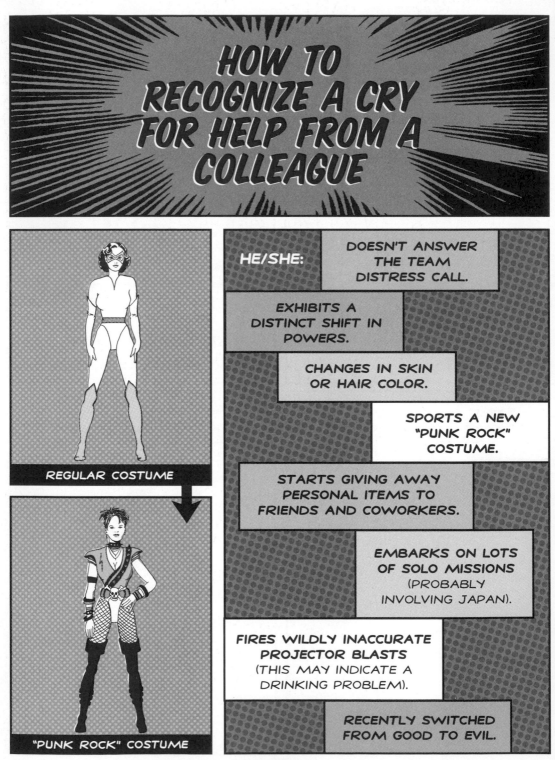

HOW TO RECOGNIZE A CRY FOR HELP FROM A COLLEAGUE

REGULAR COSTUME

"PUNK ROCK" COSTUME

HE/SHE:

DOESN'T ANSWER THE TEAM DISTRESS CALL.

EXHIBITS A DISTINCT SHIFT IN POWERS.

CHANGES IN SKIN OR HAIR COLOR.

SPORTS A NEW "PUNK ROCK" COSTUME.

STARTS GIVING AWAY PERSONAL ITEMS TO FRIENDS AND COWORKERS.

EMBARKS ON LOTS OF SOLO MISSIONS (PROBABLY INVOLVING JAPAN).

FIRES WILDLY INACCURATE PROJECTOR BLASTS (THIS MAY INDICATE A DRINKING PROBLEM).

RECENTLY SWITCHED FROM GOOD TO EVIL.

HOW TO TELL IF YOU'RE UNDER MIND CONTROL

☐ THE LITTLE VOICE IN YOUR HEAD SOUNDS DIFFERENT.

☐ YOU'RE EXPERIENCING BLACKOUTS.

☐ YOU'VE RECENTLY BEEN KIDNAPPED BY A SORCERER/
MAGUS/DEMON LORD/EGG-IMPLANTING ALIEN QUEEN.

☐ YOU'VE GONE ON A RAMPAGE AT THE WHITE HOUSE.

☐ YOU JUST DON'T FEEL LIKE YOURSELF.

☐ YOUR EYEBALLS ARE ALL SWIRLY.

EYE

SWIRLY EYE

INK BLOT TEST TO TEST FOR MIND CONTROL

THIS INK BLOT LOOKS LIKE:

A. A MAP TO MY SECRET HIDE-A-WAY

B. CAPTAIN EVIL ... WHO IS MY FRIEND

C. ME

D. A ROCKING HORSE

IF YOU ANSWER B, CONSULT YOUR MENTOR (SEE CHAPTER #10).

GETTING TO KNOW YOUR TEAMMATES

IS YOUR TEAMMATE A HOLOGRAM, ROBOT, OR CLONE?

	HOLOGRAM	ROBOT	CLONE
DOESN'T CAST A SHADOW	X		
GIVES YOU A "FUNNY FEELING"			X
TRIES TO USE LASER BEAM ON YOU		X	
SUPPOSED TO BE DEAD IN A BOX AT THE BOTTOM OF THE OCEAN	X	X	X

A note on robots: Each of these presents special challenges trust-wise, but robots are the trickiest. They can be the most loyal and upright of pals, but they are also susceptible to reprogramming, faulty control crystals, or overly literal interpretations. They also hit hard and might not always understand when you're kidding.

A note on resurrections: Resurrections are always tough to manage—perhaps you've moved on and found a new teammate/lover/nemesis, or perhaps you're unsure if your recently revived chum is the real McCoy. Ask questions involving baseball statistics or intimate birthmarks to establish his/her true identity.

50

WORKING WITH FAMILY*

Avoid discussing work at home.

Avoid discussing home at work.

Try not to engage in marital spats in front of colleagues.

Do not marry clones.**

WELL, WHOSE IDEA WAS IT TO **OPEN THE PORTAL TO THE ZERO ZONE**, ANYWAY, **MS. I-NEVER-MAKE-THE-BED-ANYMORE**?

AFTER YOU PICK UP **HORTENSE FROM THE NANNY'S**, CAN YOU STOP BY THE **HYPERBARIC PRISON CHAMBER** TO CHECK ON THE CHAMPION OF DARKNESS?

I DON'T KNOW IF I'LL BE FREE TO WORK THE **RUMMAGE SALE** ON SATURDAY, **DEAR** — I'VE GOT TO **SAVE ROMULUS IV** FROM THE RAMPAGES OF HYDROGEN MAN, **REMEMBER**?

* If you get a divorce, one of you has to leave the group or sacrifice yourself to save the other in a bittersweet act of paranormal martyrdom. This is nonnegotiable.

** If you find that you have married a clone, most jurisdictions now allow for an easy annulment.

WORKING WITH CHILDREN

Do not work with your children.

A note on children conceived in other dimensions:
If you think that your child may have been conceived in another dimension, it's important that you have him or her examined immediately, as this sort of transdimensional canoodling can lead to offspring with very unstable power surges. If the test results are positive, place your interdimensionally conceived spawn in the care of a trusted butler or peace-loving transgalactic overlord. Both would be capable of dealing with any unexpected superpower manifestations.

ARE YOU A JOINER?

Vigilantes and lone wolves generally do not do well in a team environment, whereas heroic team players thrive nicely. Where do you fall on the continuum? The Vigilante–Hero Scale represents superhero behavior as a continuum from exclusively vigilante to exclusively heroic. The continuum is excellent at showing that there are different types of heroes and it should be noted that research has indicated that only 4 percent of the superhero community falls at either end of the scale; the rest fall somewhere in between.

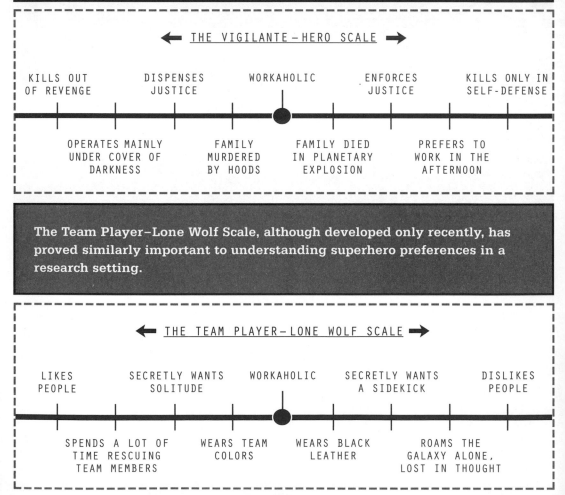

← THE VIGILANTE–HERO SCALE →

KILLS OUT OF REVENGE   DISPENSES JUSTICE   WORKAHOLIC   ENFORCES JUSTICE   KILLS ONLY IN SELF-DEFENSE

OPERATES MAINLY UNDER COVER OF DARKNESS   FAMILY MURDERED BY HOODS   FAMILY DIED IN PLANETARY EXPLOSION   PREFERS TO WORK IN THE AFTERNOON

The Team Player–Lone Wolf Scale, although developed only recently, has proved similarly important to understanding superhero preferences in a research setting.

← THE TEAM PLAYER–LONE WOLF SCALE →

LIKES PEOPLE   SECRETLY WANTS SOLITUDE   WORKAHOLIC   SECRETLY WANTS A SIDEKICK   DISLIKES PEOPLE

SPENDS A LOT OF TIME RESCUING TEAM MEMBERS   WEARS TEAM COLORS   WEARS BLACK LEATHER   ROAMS THE GALAXY ALONE, LOST IN THOUGHT

HERO

VIGILANTE

WHEN TALKING ISN'T ENOUGH

EVEN THE MOST **PROGRESSIVE ATTEMPTS** TO ACHIEVE **TEAM SELF-ACTUALIZATION** ARE NOT ALWAYS ENOUGH TO PREVENT **MISCOMMUNICATIONS**. AND WHILE EVERYONE'S BEST EFFORTS ARE IMPORTANT AND WILL OFFER SOME PROTECTION SHOULD A SUPERHEROIC PARTNERSHIP **DISSOLVE IN LITIGATION**, IT IS ADVISABLE TO TAKE FURTHER PREEMPTIVE MEASURES TO FORESTALL HURT FEELINGS AND **LARGE FINANCIAL SETTLEMENTS**.

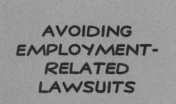
IN OUR LITIGIOUS SOCIETY, THE DISGRUNTLED OFTEN TRY TO RESOLVE THEIR GRIEVANCES THROUGH THE COURTS. AS A CRIME-FIGHTING DO-GOODER SUPERHERO, **YOU ARE MORALLY BOUND TO ACCEPT THE COURTS' JUDGMENTS,** BUT STEPS CAN BE TAKEN TO **MINIMIZE YOUR LEGAL LIABILITY** SHOULD TEAM RELATIONS GO AWRY.

Draft a contractual agreement to be signed by any prospective group member, precisely spelling out the duties and benefits inherent in membership. In addition to specifying the team bylaws, this document should dictate the team's liability in the event of various unfortunate outcomes, including (but of course not limited to) death or permanent stasis. The contract should cover:

LOSS OF POWERS
(AND EARNING ABILITY)

DESTRUCTION OR THEFT OF PERSONAL PROPERTY
(INCLUDING, BUT NOT LIMITED TO, CRIME-FIGHTING GEAR AND VEHICLES)

TEMPORARY OR PERMANENT DISABILITY
(PETRIFICATION, DIMENSIONAL EXILE, STASIS FIELDS, ETC.)

REVELATION OF SECRET IDENTITY

Specific stipulations should cover these events when they occur through the actions of a teammate, whether accidentally or through mind control. For solo heroes who are teaming up on an ad hoc basis with other solo heroes, most states do not recognize any legal or financial liability in the relationship; but, as with all things legal, the more of a paper trail you leave, the better, so it never hurts to have a spare generic Teammate Liability Contract (TLC) handy.

ESTABLISHING BYLAWS

ONE WAY TO AVOID MISCOMMUNICATION IS BY SETTING CLEAR EXPECTATIONS FROM THE OUTSET IN THE FORM OF A SET OF GROUP BYLAWS.

SUPERHERO TEAM BYLAWS (SAMPLE)

BOILERPLATE MISSION STATEMENT:

WE'RE HERE TO SERVE THE COMMON GOOD, PROTECT THE DEFENSELESS, BATTLE EVIL IN ALL ITS FORMS, ETC.

TEAM RULES:

1. THE TEAM MUST HAVE SIX (6) ACTIVE MEMBERS—HOWEVER, RESERVE MEMBER NUMBERS ARE UNLIMITED.

2. THE TEAM GUARANTEES SURVIVOR BENEFITS TBD.

3. THE TEAM WILL HAVE A ROTATING CHAIRPERSONSHIP (UNANIMOUS DECISION OR MAJORITY VOTE; TERM OF OFFICE).

4. THERE WILL BE (ABSOLUTELY) NO KILLING ON PURPOSE (EVER), UNLESS _____.

5. ALL MEMBERS MUST RESPOND TO THE ALERT BEACON IN A TIMELY MANNER.

6. EACH MEMBER WILL MAINTAIN HIS/HER PERSONAL HQ WITHIN REASONABLE DISTANCE OF TEAM HQ. ("REASONABLE" MAY BE DEFINED AS TWO [2] BLOCKS FOR A MOLASSES MUTANT OR TWO [2] CONTINENTS FOR A TELEPORTER, ETC.)

7. ALL TEAM MEMBERS WILL SHARE EQUALLY IN ANY TEAM SPIN-OFF FRANCHISING RIGHTS.

8. ALL TEAM MEMBERS WILL SHARE EQUALLY IN ALL TEAM NAME LICENSING AGREEMENTS.

9. TEAM MEMBERS HAVE A RESPONSIBILITY TO NOTIFY ALL OTHER TEAM MEMBERS IF THEIR POWERS CHANGE OR CEASE.

10. ALL TEAM MEMBERS WILL RETAIN THE RIGHT TO KEEP THEIR SECRET IDENTITIES HIDDEN FROM OTHER MEMBERS OF THE TEAM.

11. LEAVES OF ABSENCE SHALL BE GRANTED ON A CASE-BY-CASE BASIS.

12. HAZING IS NOT PERMITTED.

HEREBY SIGNED:

_____   _____

_____   _____

_____   _____

CHAPTER #7

So your parent is a **SUPER VILLAIN**. NATURALLY, THIS CAN BE **REALLY, REALLY EMBARRASSING**. WILL YOUR TEAMMATES THINK LESS OF YOU BECAUSE OF IT? **PROBABLY**. BUT THERE ARE SOME MEASURES YOU CAN TAKE TO OVERCOME YOUR **UNIQUE FAMILY BACKGROUND**. (AT LEAST YOU WEREN'T RAISED BY DOLPHINS.)

TRUST ISSUES WITH TEAMMATES

If your mother is **hell-bent** on murdering your **teammates**, you may find that your presence makes them **anxious or confused**. Are you to be trusted? Your teammates may even blame you for events that were **not** your fault at all, like that time your mother knocked the moon out of orbit, or when she trapped your colleague in subspace for nine years.

OUR FAMILY

THINGS YOU CAN DO TO MAKE YOUR TEAMMATES MORE COMFORTABLE:

PUT AWAY **FRAMED FAMILY PHOTOS.**

HOMEMADE COOKIES GO A LONG WAY.

AVOID CALLING HOME FROM HQ.

STOP REFERRING TO THE SUPER VILLAIN IN QUESTION AS "**WORLD'S GREATEST MOM.**"

You may worry that you will **go mad** or **turn evil** like your parent did. Try **not** to dwell on this. But if madness or evil does run in your family, it is advisable to **schedule an annual look-see** with a licensed psychiatrist.

DEALING WITH INSENSITIVE COWORKERS

Everyone is **embarrassed** from time to time by their parents. But no one likes having **one's family foibles** pointed out by others, and you may find that some of your colleagues are less than sensitive in their remarks. They might make off-hand comments like, "**I see that your father sank** <u>another</u> **Russian submarine.**" Use your **verbal skills** to deflect the situation.

WHEN YOUR NEMESIS IS YOUR MOM

Fighting with your mom can be awkward. Will she know your weaknesses? **If you win, can you still go home for Thanksgiving**? Just do your best in battle and remember that your mom **will kill you** if she gets the chance.

KEEPING YOUR EVIL PARENT A SECRET

Don't. The other members of the team always, always find out, and then you look like a **big jerk.**

EVIL PARENT FAQS

Q: My parent is evil. What are the chances that my child will be evil, too?

A: It is true that evil does sometimes run in families, and it has been known to skip a generation. However, this is very rare. Continue to set a positive example, and prepare a place of eternal exile for your bundle of joy, just in case.

Q: I know that my father is a super villain, but it still hurts my feelings when he tries to kill me. Is that normal?

A: Dealing with parental disapproval is hard. Sure, he's an evil megalomaniac. But he's still your dad. Try writing a letter telling him how his actions make you feel. If he still tries to kill you, consider distancing yourself. It might be that your chosen lifestyles are just not compatible.

Q: I recently found out that my mother is a super villain. What should I expect?

A: It is surprisingly common to find out late in life that one or both of your parents is evil. Perhaps you were given up for adoption at a young age. Perhaps your parent was hiding his nefarious activities from you. Either way, no one likes to find out that her parent is not who she thought he was, and the truth may take some time to sink in. Expect to experience a period of shame and anger.

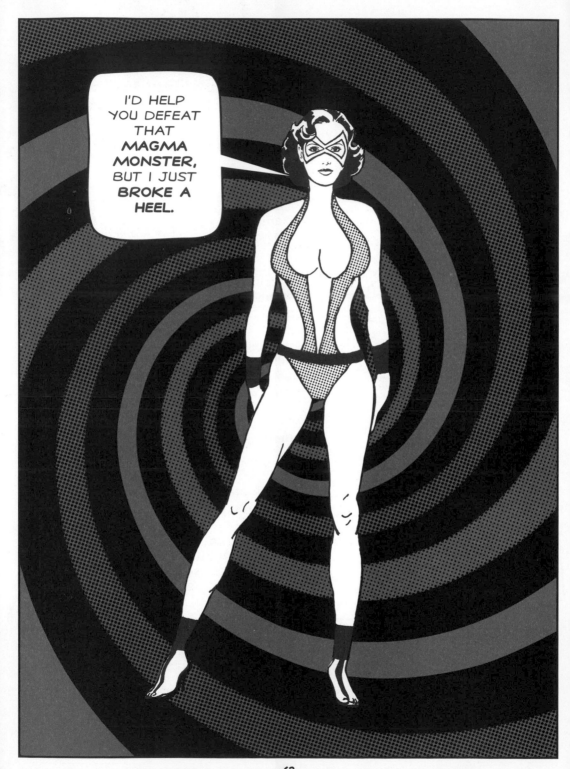

CHAPTER #8

SEXISM: IS IT STILL A PROBLEM? HOW DOES IT AFFECT YOU?

SEXISM IN THE SUPERHERO PROFESSION, AS IN MANY INDUSTRIES, HAS **DECREASED CONSIDERABLY** OVER THE PAST THIRTY YEARS. THERE WERE, HOWEVER, SOME DARK DAYS. WHILE FEMALE SUPERHEROES HAVE ALWAYS BEEN ABLE TO FIND WORK, THEY WERE USUALLY REQUIRED TO WEAR COSTUMES WITH VERY **SHORT SKIRTS** AND BOOTS WITH UNCOMFORTABLY **HIGH HEELS**. HAIRSTYLES WERE COMPLICATED AND REQUIRED CONSTANT ATTENTION, AND AN UNEXPECTEDLY DISLODGED **FALSE EYELASH** COULD CAUSE AN ENTIRE BATTLE TO **GRIND TO A HALT**. THIS WAS BEFORE TODAY'S AWARENESS OF **SEXUAL HARASSMENT** AND WOMEN HEROES PUT UP WITH MORE THAN THEIR FAIR SHARE OF INAPPROPRIATE BEHAVIOR. (IT'S HARD TO CONCENTRATE ON PREVENTING THE SUN FROM BEING EXTINGUISHED WHEN YOUR SHAPE-SHIFTER COLLEAGUE **KEEPS TURNING INTO YOUR UTILITY BELT**.) MUCH OF THIS, THANKFULLY, IS NOW BEHIND US, BUT **SEXISM DOES STILL EXIST** AND REQUIRES **ONGOING SENSITIVITY**.

TREATING FEMALE COLLEAGUES WITH RESPECT

The days are gone when the female member of your team could be left behind to "keep an eye on HQ" while the male members fought off aliens intent on earthly destruction. Some superhero teams now even have more than one female member — a gender integration almost unheard of in previous generations. These strides can be attributed to the tireless efforts of certain female superheroes in the late 1970s and early 1980s, who demanded that their powers be treated equally and insisted on being called "women" instead of "girls." *

* The achievement of Feminina and Madame Ova's joining the League of Absurdly Powerful Gentlemen should not go unmentioned.

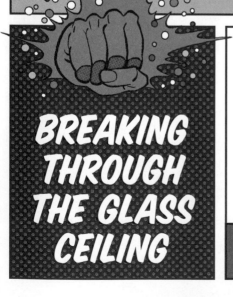

BREAKING THROUGH THE GLASS CEILING

There are still not many women in the position of team leader. But remember, just because your colleague has enormous breasts and big hair does not mean that she doesn't have what it takes to lead the team. If you are a female superhero, call your male colleagues to task if you feel that they do not take you seriously. If you feel that you've been unfairly passed over for the top spot, there are attorneys who specialize in issues relating to gender discrimination in the workplace.

Note: Ladies, you can help the cause by not insisting on being called "Princess" unless you actually *are* a princess.

SEXISM AND COSTUME CHOICE

IF YOUR COLLEAGUE CHOOSES TO WEAR A COSTUME CONSISTING OF TINY BANDS OF STRATEGICALLY PLACED LYCRA, ASSUME THIS IS BECAUSE IT IS COMFORTABLE AND EASY TO JUMP AROUND IN AND NOT BECAUSE SHE IS TARTY. YOU MAY FIND IT DIFFICULT TO AVOID STARING AT HER EXPOSED DÉCOLLETAGE, BUT SHE WILL APPRECIATE IT IF YOU MAINTAIN EYE CONTACT.

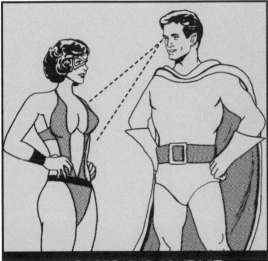

IMPROPER EYE CONTACT

PROPER EYE CONTACT

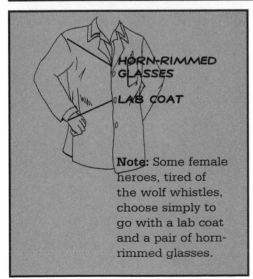

HORN-RIMMED GLASSES

LAB COAT

Note: Some female heroes, tired of the wolf whistles, choose simply to go with a lab coat and a pair of horn-rimmed glasses.

DISCUSSION QUESTION:

YOU FIND THAT YOUR MALE TEAMMATES ARE HOLDING BACK IN BATTLE. WHEN CONFRONTED, THEY SAY THAT YOU'RE "DOING FINE" AND JUST WANT TO "WATCH YOU IN ACTION." YOU SUSPECT THEY HAVE OTHER MOTIVATIONS.

WHAT SHOULD YOU DO?

CHAPTER #9

UNDERSTANDING YOUR NEMESIS

YOUR RELATIONSHIP WITH YOUR NEMESIS MAY BE THE **MOST IMPORTANT RELATIONSHIP** YOU HAVE AS A SUPERHERO. DON'T TAKE IT CASUALLY. SOME HEROES MAINTAIN RELATIONSHIPS WITH THREE TO FIVE PRIMARY NEMESES OVER THE PERIOD OF THEIR CAREERS. THIS **LEVEL OF COMMITMENT** MAY SEEM DAUNTING, BUT HAVING A LONG-TERM NEMESIS CAN ALLOW FOR A LEVEL OF MUTUAL UNDERSTANDING THAT **BACK-ALLEY PICKUP BATTLES** WITH VILLAINS LOOKING FOR A QUICK **THRILL** CANNOT APPROXIMATE.

WHAT YOUR CHOICE OF NEMESIS SAYS ABOUT YOU

1. IS HE SMARTER THAN YOU ARE?

It may be possible that you have chosen a brainiac villain because of your own intellectual insecurities. Many superheroes start their careers as teenagers and forsake college for advanced judo training. If you are worried about your intellectual prowess, consider attending some community college classes or undertaking a regular crossword-puzzle regimen.

BRAINIAC NEMESIS = INTELLECTUAL INSECURITIES.

2. IS HE IMMORTAL?

Having an immortal nemesis can be very, very challenging. How do you stop someone who cannot be killed or physically injured? Perhaps it is this Sisyphean scenario that appeals to you in the first place. Ask yourself, Am I afraid of winning? If so, why? Maybe you feel that you don't deserve to win. Address this issue with a licensed psychiatrist.

IMMORTAL NEMESIS = FEAR OF SUCCESS.

3. IS SHE MORE ATTRACTIVE THAN YOU ARE?

Is your nemesis impossibly ravishing and always stylishly dressed? Does she even know you exist? Consider the possibility that she may be out of your league. If your nemesis won't even respond to your entrées into battles, you might want to take a long, hard look in the mirror and ask yourself if she's the right fiendishly evil woman for you. Be realistic.

SUPERHOT NEMESIS = INFLATED SENSE OF SELF-WORTH.

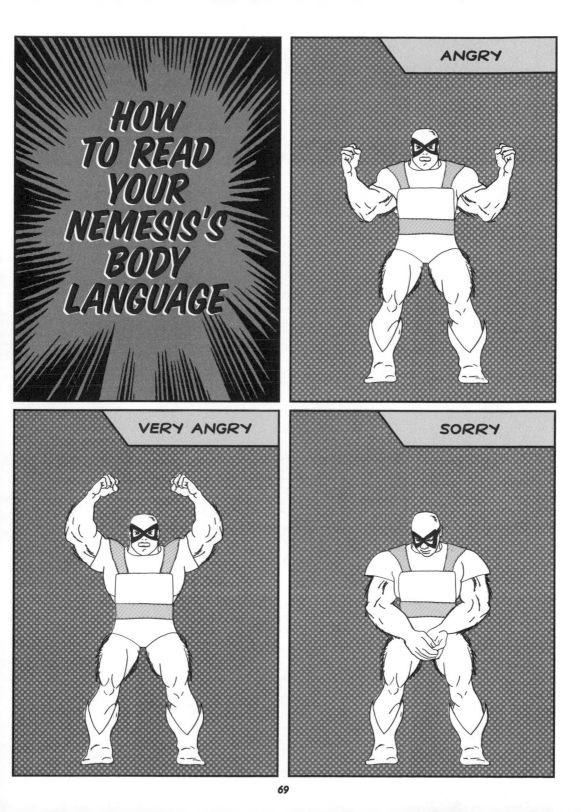

HONESTY AND INTEGRITY WHEN DEALING WITH YOUR NEMESIS

YOU AND YOUR TEAM MEMBERS FINALLY LOCATE THE SECRET LAIR OF YOUR NEMESIS. BUT BY THE TIME YOU ARRIVE, HE HAS ALREADY DISPOSED OF HIS CACHE OF ANTIMATTER. HE LAUGHS AT YOU, SAYING, **"HEY MAN, LOOK AROUND — YOU GOT NOTHING. YOU'RE NOTHING! YOU CAN'T EVEN ARREST ME!"** YOU SEARCH HIS LAIR THOROUGHLY AND INDEED COME UP WITH NO EVIDENCE OF HIS DASTARDLY PLAN. SHOULD YOU:

A BEGIN CARRYING SMALL AMOUNTS OF ANTIMATTER TO PLANT ON KNOWN VILLAINS IN THE FUTURE?

B ARREST YOUR NEMESIS AND TAKE HIM TO YOUR HQ FOR INTERROGATION JUST TO SPITE HIM?

C RUN CELLOPHANE TAPE OVER HIS HANDS, AND RUN IT THROUGH THE SUPERCOMPUTER AT HQ TO SEARCH FOR MICROSCOPIC EVIDENCE OF ANTIMATTER?

ANSWER: C. (ANSWERS A AND B, WHILE TEMPORARILY REWARDING, ARE AGAINST THE SUPERHERO CODE OF CONDUCT, AND IF DISCOVERED WOULD MOST LIKELY RESULT IN STRESS-RELATED ILLNESS, IF NOT OUTRIGHT INTERGALACTIC DISBARMENT.)

ALLYING WITH ONE ENEMY IN ORDER TO DEFEAT ANOTHER

THERE MAY COME A TIME WHEN YOU FIND YOURSELF FACED WITH A DIFFICULT DILEMMA: DO YOU JOIN FORCES WITH "ENEMY A" IN ORDER TO DEFEAT "ENEMY B"? ASK YOURSELF THE FOLLOWING QUESTIONS: IS "ENEMY B" A GREATER THREAT THAN "ENEMY A"? IS "ENEMY B" A MORE IMMINENT THREAT THAN "ENEMY A"?

These calculations can become complex. If some two-bit creep with a power suit has captured your elderly aunt, and a horribly disfigured wealthy industrialist offers to help you rescue her, but only in exchange for the positronic neutralizer you confiscated from him last year, well, you're in a pickle. **Ask yourself—is there any other way to rescue your elderly aunt without providing this dangerous weapon to such a global threat?** *

Other situations may be subtler. Your sidekick is suffering from acute space sickness, and only the evilest doctor in the galaxy (ironically, your old college roommate) has the cure. He may offer it to you with no strings (seemingly) attached. This ploy is used by villains who just want to "get into your head" or be able to call in a favor down the road. **Consider the emotional cost of such a bargain against the benefits of a healthy sidekick. Only you can make this call.**

* **There usually is.**

INTIMIDATION IS A TWO-WAY STREET

Sometimes the best way to defeat evil is simply to stare it down. Metal face plates, insect or lightning bolt insignias, and little devil horns or bat ears may prove useful in your attempt to out-intimidate your opponent.

The bigger bully the villain is, the more likely he will be susceptible to counter-intimidation. Stone aliens from Saturn are particularly susceptible to this sort of psychological terrorizing. When dealing with technology-dependent villains, focus on disabling their battle suits or cyber whips. You'll be amazed at how quickly their posturing collapses once they've been disarmed.

METAL FACEPLATE

INSECT OR LIGHTNING BOLT INSIGNIA

BAT EARS

LITTLE DEVIL HORNS

Note: Refer to your favorite nemesis as your "arch nemesis." This will irritate him and prove distracting in battle.

NEMESIS SHOPPING

IT'S TEMPTING TO TRY TO **LAND A NEMESIS** WHOSE VERY NAME **STRIKES FEAR** IN THE HEARTS OF EVEN THE MOST **RIGHTEOUS OF HEROES**. IT MAY ALSO BE TEMPTING TO FIND A NEMESIS WHO IS JUST STARTING OUT AND MAY BE **EASILY COWED**. BOTH SCENARIOS WILL MAKE YOU FEEL BETTER ABOUT YOURSELF FOR A WHILE, BUT THE FACT OF THE MATTER IS, YOU ARE BEST OFF CHOOSING A NEMESIS WHO IS **IN YOUR CLASS**. DO YOUR RESEARCH! KNOW YOUR NEMESIS. THE FOLLOWING NEMESIS/POWER CHART CAN HELP.

NEMESIS/POWER CHART

	THE POWER OF THE COSMOS	STORM-CONJURING	SUPERSONIC FLIGHT	MAGIC	SUPER STRENGTH	SUPER INTELLECT	INVISIBILITY	IMPERVIOUSNESS TO PAIN	ÜBER PHEROMONES	TELEPATHY	MOLECULAR MANIPULATION	TELEKINESIS	TRICKED-OUT COSTUME	RAY OF HEAT/FROST/ELECTRICITY, ETC.	LOTS OF DOUGH	VICIOUS SNEER
IMMORTAL ELDER OF THE UNIVERSE	X	X	X	X	X	X	X	X	X	X	X	X		X		X
MYTHOLOGICAL GOD	X	X	X	X	X	X			X		X	X	X	X		X
EVIL SUPER-GENIUS						X				X			X		X	X
INTERSTELLAR SHAPE-SHIFTER						X	X	X			X					X
GIANT ROBOT			X		X			X						X		X
MAGMA MONSTER		X			X			X			X			X		X
WIZARD		X		X		X	X		X	X	X	X	X	X		X
NORMAL-SIZE ROBOT								X						X		X
NAZI WAR CRIMINAL						X		X					X		X	X
PSYCHOTIC CEO						X		X					X		X	X
ALIEN			X		X	X							X	X		X
MOLE MAN								X								X
CONJURED BEAST				X	X			X						X		X
CRIMINAL ENTREPRENEUR						X			X				X		X	X
MAFIA LOAN SHARK						X		X							X	X
HEAD OF ROGUE STATE								X					X		X	X
TINY ROBOT								X								X
PETTY HOOD																X
VANDAL																X

CHAPTER #10

THE RIGHT MENTOR IS HARD TO FIND

THE MENTOR-MENTEE RELATION-SHIP IS A DELICATE **PAS DE DEUX** AND MUST BE TAKEN **VERY SERIOUSLY**. A GOOD MENTOR CAN BE AN INVALUABLE RESOURCE. A BAD MENTOR CAN **WREAK HAVOC** ON A SUPERHERO'S **FRAGILE PSYCHE**.

Note: While we're on the topic, let's take a moment to distinguish the mentor-mentee relationship from the superhero-sidekick relationship, as they are often confused. A mentor is always there for you, even once you're an independent hero of your own. You can always call on them for a bit of advice, though they rarely will accompany you on adventures. When a sidekick hooks up with a hero, he is entering into a relationship that is generally assumed to be temporary, with the expectation that the sidekick will eventually go his or her own way. The level of instruction and oversight of a sidekick is therefore much more intensive and specific than that of a protégé.

WHAT TO LOOK FOR IN A MENTOR

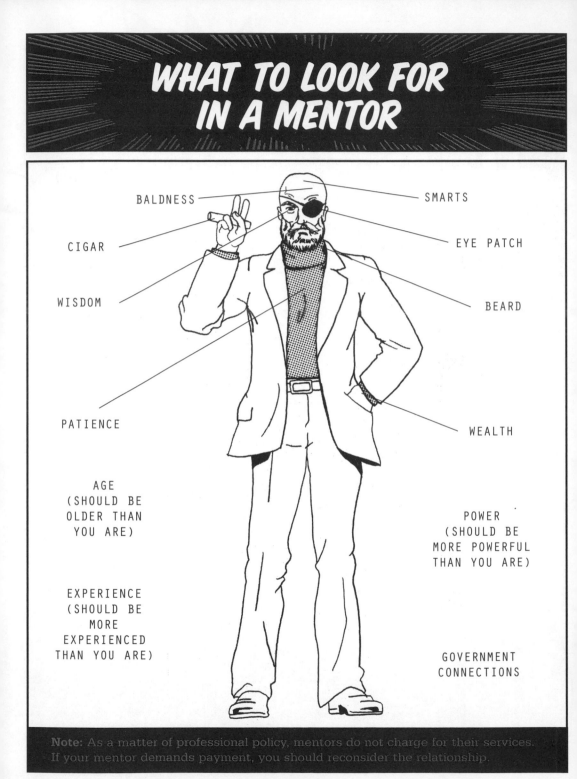

BALDNESS

SMARTS

CIGAR

EYE PATCH

WISDOM

BEARD

PATIENCE

WEALTH

AGE
(SHOULD BE
OLDER THAN
YOU ARE)

POWER
(SHOULD BE
MORE POWERFUL
THAN YOU ARE)

EXPERIENCE
(SHOULD BE
MORE
EXPERIENCED
THAN YOU ARE)

GOVERNMENT
CONNECTIONS

Note: As a matter of professional policy, mentors do not charge for their services. If your mentor demands payment, you should reconsider the relationship.

BREAKING FREE FROM A DYSFUNCTIONAL MENTOR RELATIONSHIP

Some mentors are righteous defenders of the good who are simply a bit past their prime. While this puts them in an excellent position to pass their wisdom along to the next generation, some mentors may experience feelings of resentment and even anger over their perceived decline and looming mortality. This doesn't excuse their flaws, but recognizing the origins of these emotions may help you deal with them when they arise. If you sense that the relationship may be souring, it is best to sever it quickly so that you may begin the healing process.

TROUBLE SIGNS

YOUR MENTOR DISAPPEARS FOR YEARS AT A TIME.

YOUR MENTOR NEVER TAKES YOU TO THE NEGATIVE ZONE.

YOUR MENTOR TRIES TO KILL YOU.

YOUR MENTOR DOES TOO MUCH FOR YOU (ALWAYS STEPPING IN).

YOUR MENTOR GIVES ADVICE, BUT IT IS ALWAYS ACCOMPANIED BY EXASPERATED SIGHS.

YOUR MENTOR HOGS THE GLORY.

YOU MENTOR KEEPS TRYING TO DITCH YOU.

YOUR MENTOR IS CONSTANTLY TELLING STORIES ABOUT HIS FORMER PROTÉGÉS' EXPLOITS.

YOUR MENTOR WON'T RETURN YOUR CALLS.

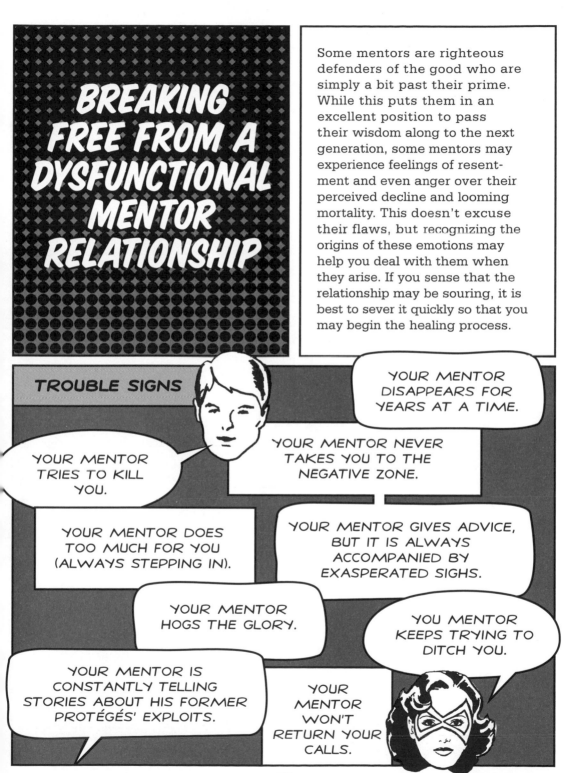

HOW TO FIND A MENTOR

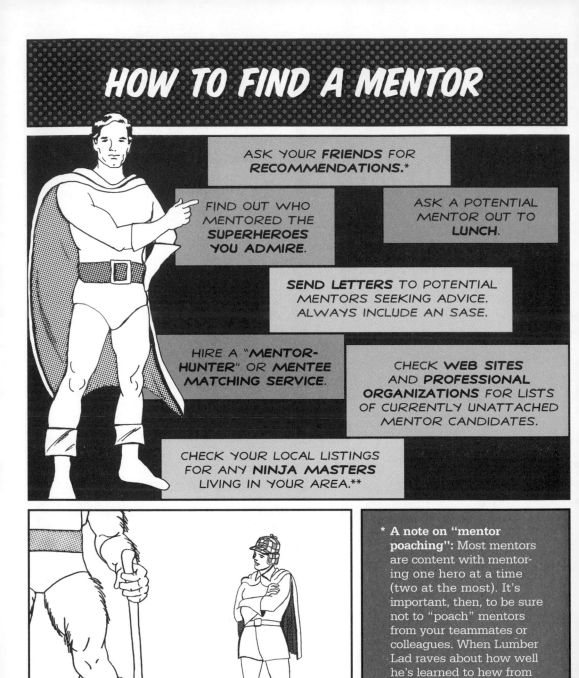

ASK YOUR **FRIENDS** FOR **RECOMMENDATIONS.***

FIND OUT WHO MENTORED THE **SUPERHEROES YOU ADMIRE.**

ASK A POTENTIAL MENTOR OUT TO **LUNCH.**

SEND LETTERS TO POTENTIAL MENTORS SEEKING ADVICE. ALWAYS INCLUDE AN SASE.

HIRE A "**MENTOR-HUNTER**" OR MENTEE MATCHING SERVICE.

CHECK **WEB SITES** AND **PROFESSIONAL ORGANIZATIONS** FOR LISTS OF CURRENTLY UNATTACHED MENTOR CANDIDATES.

CHECK YOUR LOCAL LISTINGS FOR ANY **NINJA MASTERS** LIVING IN YOUR AREA.**

* **A note on "mentor poaching":** Most mentors are content with mentoring one hero at a time (two at the most). It's important, then, to be sure not to "poach" mentors from your teammates or colleagues. When Lumber Lad raves about how well he's learned to hew from Captain Bunyan, that's not necessarily an invitation to approach Bunyan about becoming *your* mentor.

** Avoid evil ninja cults.

OVERCOMING MENTOR ENVY

No matter where you are in your career, it's perfectly normal to feel **insecure about your mentor**. It is inevitable that you will meet other superheroes who will seem to have **bigger, better mentors** than yours. Don't let yourself get caught up in **petty jealousies**. If your mentor is a good fit for you, that's all that matters. Don't let others make you feel bad just because your mentor looks or acts differently from theirs.

Some less-mature heroes may try to feed your insecurities with taunts such as "*My* mentor, Lord Ultimate, can incinerate 3.6 gigaliters of nuclear waste before prevailing winds disperse it over Los Angeles. I heard *your* mentor, Reptilicus, had to be rescued after his skin dried out." These **nattering nellies** are just jealous and are **looking for attention**. Their empty jeers can't hurt you unless you give them power.

DISCUSSION QUESTION

YOU HAVE AN OPPORTUNITY TO STUDY WITH AN ESTEEMED MENTOR, BUT SHE LIVES IN ANOTHER DIMENSION.

DO YOU COMMUTE?

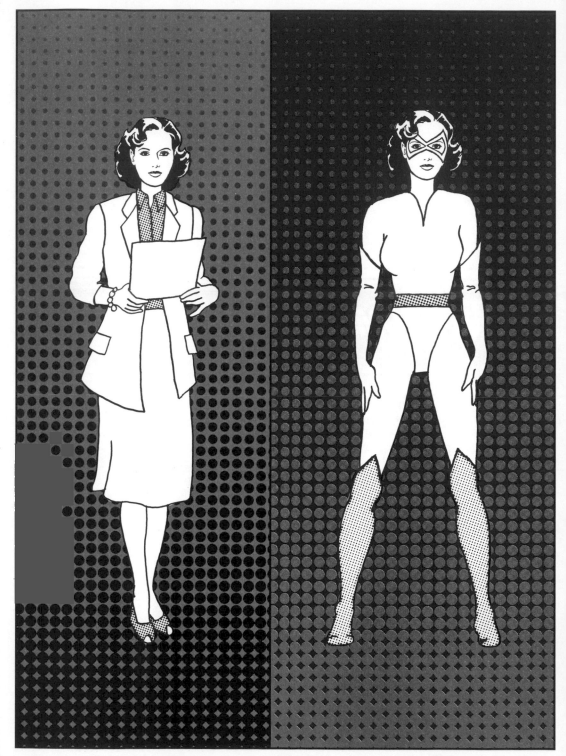

CHAPTER #11

SECRET IDENTITY CRISES

THERE ARE FEW **MENTAL STRAINS** AS STRESSFUL AS THE EFFORT TO **MAINTAIN A SECRET IDENTITY.** MANY A SUPERHERO HAS GONE OFF HER NUT TRYING TO **KEEP UP A HOME IN WESTCHESTER** WHILE ALSO **SAVING THE EASTERN SEABOARD** FROM MOLE PEOPLE. IT'S OK TO FEEL OVERWHELMED. SOME SMART DECISIONS EARLY ON CAN HELP LIMIT ANY **PSYCHO-LOGICAL COMPLICATIONS.**

NO SECRET VS. SECRET IDENTITY*

NO SECRET IDENTITY	SECRET IDENTITY
FAME	PRIVACY
CAREFREE	MUST MAINTAIN COVER
ENEMIES KNOW WHO YOU ARE	ENEMIES DON'T KNOW WHO YOU ARE
NO NEED FOR CRAPPY COVER JOB	MUST HAVE CRAPPY COVER JOB
NO MASK	MASK
LOVED ONES IN DANGER	LOVED ONES LIED TO
AUTOGRAPH SEEKERS	BILL COLLECTORS
GOVERNMENT COOPERATION	GOVERNMENT HARASSMENT

* Naturally, not all superheroes have the option of a secret identity. If you are ten feet tall and made of shingles, it may prove difficult to "pass" in the workaday world, though you can always camouflage yourself as a roof.

NEGOTIATING YOUR SECRET IDENTITY AT WORK

PERHAPS YOU HAVE CHOSEN TO CARRY ON A SECRET IDENTITY. PERHAPS NOT. IF YOU HAVE, THAT DOES NOT AUTO-MATICALLY MEAN THAT YOU ARE A **DECEIVING, CONFLICTED BORDERLINE PERSONALITY**. MANY SUPERHEROES MAINTAIN PERFECTLY HEALTHY SECRET LIVES AND ARE THE BETTER FOR IT. THERE IS NO SINGLE TRICK TO ACHIEVING THIS GOAL, BUT THERE ARE SOME **IMPORTANT STEPS** YOU CAN TAKE TO ENSURE THAT YOU HAVE A CHANCE.

YOUR "JOB"

Most likely your secret identity requires that you maintain some sort of job. It's a hassle, but there you have it. Please note that some jobs are more compatible with the superhero lifestyle than others (see table). If you find that you are unhappy or conflicted in your job, you might want to consider exploring a new field.

COMMON PROFESSIONS FOR SUPERHEROES*

PROFESSIONS	QUALIFICATIONS	EGGHEAD	ATHLETIC	ARTY	INDEPENDENTLY WEALTHY	EXCEPTIONALLY GOOD LOOKING
GENETICIST		X				
APPRENTICE SORCERER		X		X		
CIRCUS PERFORMER			X	X		
STUDENT		X				
BRILLIANT SURGEON		X				X
FINANCIER		X			X	
INDUSTRIALIST					X	
FASHION MODEL						X
PART-TIME SALES CLERK					X	X
JOURNALIST		X		X		
NUCLEAR LABORATORY TECHNICIAN		X				
NUCLEAR PHYSICIST		X				
VULCANOLOGIST		X	X			
TEST PILOT			X			
BOUNTY HUNTER			X			X
TEACHER		X				
CONSTRUCTION WORKER			X			X
SPY		X	X	X	X	X
PRIVATE INVESTIGATOR			X			
SECRETARY						X
SOCIALITE					X	X
PROFESSOR		X				
ILLUSTRATOR				X		
ROCK STAR						X
LAWYER		X				

* If possible, freelance or be your own boss. Also consider taking on a trusted assistant or law partner who can handle things when you're out of the office.

WHEN IS IT APPROPRIATE TO USE YOUR SUPERPOWERS IN THE WORKPLACE?

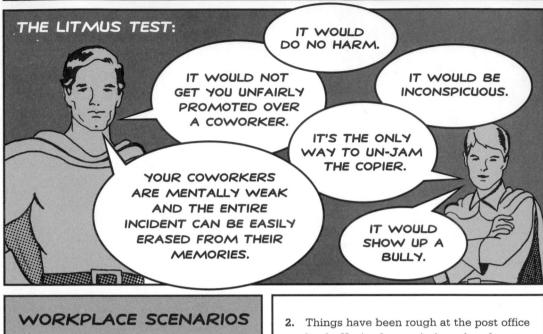

THE LITMUS TEST:

IT WOULD DO NO HARM.

IT WOULD NOT GET YOU UNFAIRLY PROMOTED OVER A COWORKER.

IT WOULD BE INCONSPICUOUS.

IT'S THE ONLY WAY TO UN-JAM THE COPIER.

YOUR COWORKERS ARE MENTALLY WEAK AND THE ENTIRE INCIDENT CAN BE EASILY ERASED FROM THEIR MEMORIES.

IT WOULD SHOW UP A BULLY.

WORKPLACE SCENARIOS

1. The new junior partner at your law firm, Carl, thinks he's God's gift to women, and Mindy, the beautiful blonde receptionist, whom you've had your eye on for a while, seems especially receptive to his oily charms. You should:

(a) Use you ability to alter the molecular makeup of any substance on his smug face.
(b) Use your power to turn Mindy's stapler into a bouquet of flowers and ask her out.
(c) Wait until the first time you see them kiss, then make their faces stick together forever, if that's what they want so bad.
(d) None of the above.

2. Things have been rough at the post office lately. You've been missing a lot of routes recently due to the ongoing transgalactic battle between the Snerds and the Caalien Empire. Hank, your rival and coworker, seems poised to get the supervisor's position you're after. And every time the gang goes out after work for drinks, you end up at some lousy sports bar where you feel awkward. You should:

(a) Subtly manipulate the mind of your boss with a Soul Whisper to convince him to patronize a less heinous watering hole.
(b) Take advantage of your super-strength to hurl Hank into a black hole.
(c) Focus an ion blast at the core of Alpha Centauri, causing it to go supernova and decimate both warring space species.
(d) All of the above.

Answers: 1: d; 2: a.

SECRET IDENTITIES AND RELATIONSHIPS

AFTER ONE YEAR — AND A THOROUGH BACKGROUND CHECK.

ONCE YOU'VE BEEN CONFRONTED.

TO SAVE A LIFE.

IF YOU THINK HE OR SHE CAN'T HANDLE IT AND YOU'RE LOOKING FOR A REASON TO BREAK UP.

POTENTIAL RELATIONSHIP CONFLICTS

Issues of trust and reliability.

Boyfriends/girlfriends can have a keen sense of when they are being lied to.

Your significant other may feel like you don't value him/her that much, since you're always missing birthday parties, dates, anniversaries, etc.

RESENTMENT

YOU MIGHT FEEL RESENTFUL. THE SO-CALLED DECEPTION IS ALL FOR YOUR BOYFRIEND'S OWN GOOD, BUT HE IS **TOO SELFISH** AND **PATHOLOGICALLY NEEDY** TO SEE THAT. YOU DIDN'T ASK TO GET HIT BY THAT **SUBAQUATIC RAY** AND **GET TURNED INTO THE CRAB,** AND ALL YOU'RE TRYING TO DO IS DEAL, IN THE BEST WAY YOU CAN, WITH A SITUATION THAT WOULD PROBABLY DRIVE MOST PEOPLE NUTS, AND IF THAT MEANS MISLEADING THE ONE YOU LOVE, THEN SO BE IT. HE CAN TAKE HIS CIVILIAN BUTT BACK TO HOBOKEN IF HE DOESN'T LIKE IT.

Note on bad breakups: It is a sad truth that the boyfriends/girlfriends/spouses of superheroes have a way of getting themselves killed by the forces of evil, falling to their deaths, committing suicide, or simply going mad. After your fourth wife gets disintegrated by a solar blaster, it's not abnormal to wonder, "Is it me?" Don't second-guess yourself. It's not your fault.

IDENTITY CRISIS

THE PRESSURES OF MAINTAINING A DUAL IDENTITY CAN LEAD TO AN **IDENTITY CRISIS**. THERE ARE TWO SIDES TO THIS PROBLEM. EITHER YOU'RE **BORN WITH SUPERPOWERS** (ALIEN, MUTANT, ETC.) AND YOU HAVE TO CONSTRUCT A FALSE CIVILIAN IDENTITY FOR COVER, OR YOU ARE A **CIVILIAN WHO GAINS POWERS** AND ALREADY HAS AN IDENTITY TO PRESERVE. EITHER WAY, YOU ARE NOW, IN SOME PART OF YOUR LIFE, LIVING A LIE. THE FACT THAT **YOU CAN'T BE YOURSELF AROUND THE PEOPLE WHO LOVE YOU** WILL INEVITABLY LEAD TO **FEELINGS OF GUILT AND FRUSTRATION.** BUT SOMETIMES THAT'S JUST PART OF WEARING THE CAPE.

POTENTIAL RELATIONSHIP CONFLICTS

FOLLOWING THE CONFESSION OF YOUR TRUE IDENTITY, YOUR GIRLFRIEND/BOYFRIEND MAY BECOME JEALOUS OF YOUR RACY COSTUMED TEAMMATES.

HE/SHE MAY EXHIBIT EXCEPTIONAL FEAR FOR YOUR SAFETY.*

HE/SHE MAY CRITICIZE YOUR CRIME-FIGHTING TECHNIQUE.

HE/SHE MAY TURN OUT TO BE A VILLAIN.

* The last thing you need is the love of your life showing up in the middle of your big bridge battle to make sure you get home safe.

MOST SIGNIFICANT OTHERS, ONCE THEY GET OVER THEIR FEAR, ARE **INTENSELY SUPPORTIVE**, BUT SOME MAY HARBOR JEALOUSIES OVER YOUR EXCITING LIFESTYLE, POWER RING, OR ABILITY TO FLY. THIS ENVY MAY EXPRESS ITSELF THROUGH **CUTTING COMMENTS** ABOUT **SMALL FAILURES**. IF YOU FIND THAT THIS CONSTANT NEGATIVITY IS DAMAGING YOUR SELF-ESTEEM, TALK TO YOUR LOVED ONE ABOUT HIS/HER RESENTMENT. SOMETIMES AN EXTRA UNITARD AND A BIT OF BEDROOM SUPERHERO-PLAY CAN TEMPORARILY **DEFUSE** THESE FESTERING ISSUES.

If you are an alien, you may find yourself especially anxious when in your secret identity. It's only natural that you'll feel more comfortable in your original shape and around others who share your background. Remember to take off your human suit several times a day, especially in the summer when it can get stuffy.

DATING OTHER SUPERHEROES

IT'S ONLY NATURAL TO FORM CLOSE BONDS WITH YOUR COWORKERS. SOMETIMES THESE BONDS LEAD TO **AFFAIRS OF THE HEART**. AND SOMETIMES, THESE WORKPLACE ROMANCES TRANSITION INTO LONG-LASTING MARRIAGES. BUT MORE OFTEN THEY LEAD ONLY TO **AWKWARDNESS AND HEARTBREAK**. IN THE SUPERHERO WORLD, THEY MAY EVEN LEAD TO PLANETARY CRISIS (OR AT LEAST THE DESTRUCTION OF A FEW SQUARE CITY BLOCKS).

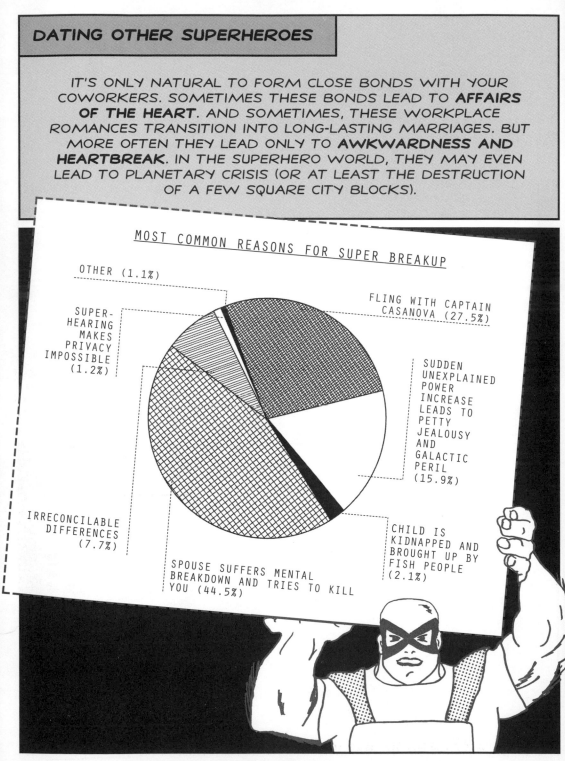

MOST COMMON REASONS FOR SUPER BREAKUP

OTHER (1.1%)

SUPER-HEARING MAKES PRIVACY IMPOSSIBLE (1.2%)

FLING WITH CAPTAIN CASANOVA (27.5%)

SUDDEN UNEXPLAINED POWER INCREASE LEADS TO PETTY JEALOUSY AND GALACTIC PERIL (15.9%)

IRRECONCILABLE DIFFERENCES (7.7%)

CHILD IS KIDNAPPED AND BROUGHT UP BY FISH PEOPLE (2.1%)

SPOUSE SUFFERS MENTAL BREAKDOWN AND TRIES TO KILL YOU (44.5%)

Q: I'm in love with my superhero colleague, and he won't tell me his real name. Does this indicate a lack of trust?

A: There's no better indication of trust than a hero's willingness to reveal his or her secret identity, and the sharing of a secret identity can be a significant milestone in a relationship. Still, some heroes have solid reasons for keeping their civilian lives to themselves, such as wanting to maintain that all-important air of mystery in the relationship, or simply fearing that you may be turned off by their mundane "real" life as a construction worker. Of course, they could also be keeping a secret double life from you that includes kids and a duplex in suburban Pittsburgh. Beware especially of entering relationships with heroes named Sergeant Cad, The Heart Breaker, or Black Valentine.

Q: I'm in love with Thunder Man, but I'm not so crazy about his socially awkward, cowardly, myopic alter ego, Dr. Willard Pitt. Is it wrong to insist that he "put on the cape" whenever we go out?

A: As everyone who has ever been in a relationship knows, there are always some aspects about our loved ones that we like more than others. We simply choose to tolerate those less-appealing characteristics as part of the whole package. You may enjoy Thunder Man more when he is in his loincloth and cape than when he is hunchbacked and wearing his lab coat, but keep in mind that he wants to be loved for who he really is, not how his costume fits. Try developing common interests, like string theory or beaker collecting.

PROTECTING YOUR SECRET IDENTITY AT ALL COSTS

If you are going to maintain a secret identity, it is very important that you learn how to fool people. Deception and distraction may prove useful.

CONSIDER FAKING (OR ACTUALLY DEVELOPING) A PHYSICAL CONDITION THAT WOULD AUTOMATICALLY RULE YOU OUT AS A SUPERHERO IN PEOPLE'S MINDS, SUCH AS:

A LIMP

BLINDNESS

DEAFNESS

NEARSIGHTEDNESS

YOUTH

A PONYTAIL

USEFUL TERMS

Being made:
Recognition of a superhero by a civilian.

Being burned:
Another term for being recognized by a civilian.

Blown cover:
What you have when you've been made.

Cover story:
A lie.

HOW TO CONCEAL THE TRUTH BEHIND THE MYSTERIOUS WOUNDS

Develop a reputation as a klutz or sleepwalker.

Use hypnosis or illusion powers.

Find a dependable facial base makeup.

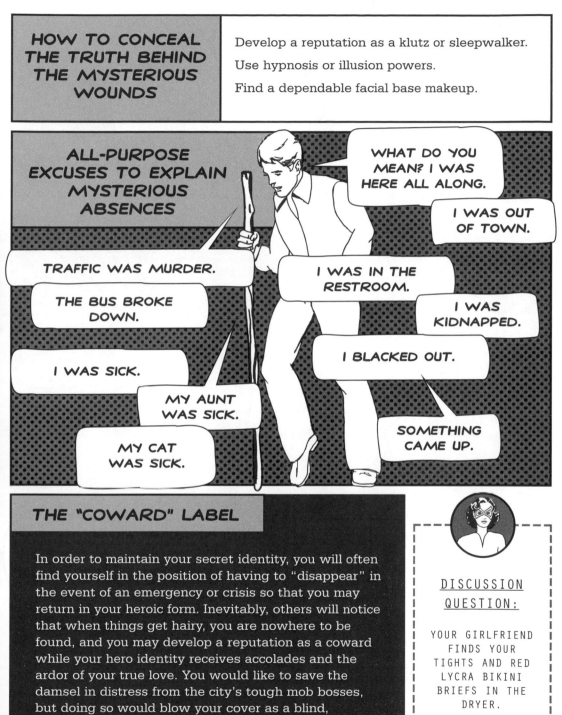

ALL-PURPOSE EXCUSES TO EXPLAIN MYSTERIOUS ABSENCES

WHAT DO YOU MEAN? I WAS HERE ALL ALONG.

I WAS OUT OF TOWN.

TRAFFIC WAS MURDER.

THE BUS BROKE DOWN.

I WAS IN THE RESTROOM.

I WAS KIDNAPPED.

I WAS SICK.

I BLACKED OUT.

MY AUNT WAS SICK.

MY CAT WAS SICK.

SOMETHING CAME UP.

THE "COWARD" LABEL

In order to maintain your secret identity, you will often find yourself in the position of having to "disappear" in the event of an emergency or crisis so that you may return in your heroic form. Inevitably, others will notice that when things get hairy, you are nowhere to be found, and you may develop a reputation as a coward while your hero identity receives accolades and the ardor of your true love. You would like to save the damsel in distress from the city's tough mob bosses, but doing so would blow your cover as a blind, wheelchair-bound assistant accountant.

DISCUSSION QUESTION:

YOUR GIRLFRIEND FINDS YOUR TIGHTS AND RED LYCRA BIKINI BRIEFS IN THE DRYER.

WHAT DO YOU DO?

CHAPTER #12

COSTUMES AND BODY IMAGE

THERE IS GROWING PEER PRESSURE AMONG SUPERHEROES TO **DIET AND EXERCISE** TO AN UNHEALTHY DEGREE. MEDIA AND ADVERTISING IMAGES PROMOTE AN **UNATTAINABLE SUPERHERO IDEAL**, AND THE SUPERHERO COMMUNITY IS AWASH IN FAD DIETS AND WEIGHT-LOSS PROGRAMS. THE EXISTENCE OF **HEROES WITH SUPER METABOLISMS** AND **ALIEN OR GENETICALLY ENGINEERED PHYSIQUES** HASN'T HELPED MATTERS, AS SUCH HEROES HAVE SET AN UNATTAINABLE STANDARD. SINCE THERE IS A CULTURAL TENDENCY TO JUDGE PEOPLE BY THEIR APPEARANCE, IT IS NO SURPRISE THAT THE PUBLIC DEMANDS A "PERFECT" FORM FROM ITS SUPERHEROES. THE **HOST OF BODY-IMAGE ISSUES** IS ONLY CONFOUNDED BY THE **UNFORGIVING NATURE** OF THE AVERAGE SUPERHERO ENSEMBLE.

LEARNING TO LOVE YOUR BODY

TIPS FOR IMPROVING YOUR BODY IMAGE

STOP WEIGHING YOURSELF. (ESPECIALLY IF YOU'RE MADE OF SOLID ROCK OR HEAVY METAL.)

FOCUS ON IMPROVING YOUR HEALTH, RATHER THAN ON IMPROVING YOUR PHYSIQUE.

REFLECT ON YOUR CHILDHOOD AND ATTEMPT TO UNEARTH THE ROOT CAUSES OF YOUR BODY-IMAGE ISSUES.

ACCEPT THE FACT THAT YOU WILL ALWAYS WEIGH MORE THAN AIR GIRL.

TALK ABOUT YOUR FEELINGS.

I HAVE A PH.D.

IS MY COSTUME RIGHT FOR ME?

COMPLETE THE FOLLOWING MULTIPLE-CHOICE SENTENCES:

1. MY COSTUME MAKES ME FEEL [FAT, POWERFUL, SILLY, LIKE A STRUMPET].

2. IT TAKES ME [5 SECONDS, 30 SECONDS, 1 MINUTE, A NANOFLASH] TO DON MY COSTUME.

3. MY BEST FEATURE IS MY [TORSO, FORELOCK, EYES, PERSONALITY].

4. I SPEND MOST OF MY COSTUME BUDGET ON [BOOTS, COWL, MY ENCHANTED BELT OF STRENGTH, STICKUM].

5. IN COSTUME, THE OUTLINE OF MY TORSO RESEMBLES [AN INVERTED PYRAMID, AN HOURGLASS, A ROCK PILE, NEBRASKA].

6. IN PUBLIC, MY APPEARANCE DRAWS [LEERS, SMIRKING AND POINTING, CRYPTOZOOLOGISTS, A FINE].

7. I'M ALWAYS TRYING TO COVER MY [FREQUENT DISAPPEARANCES, TEAMMATES, FACE, CELLULITE].

WELL, HOW DOES THIS MAKE YOU FEEL?

CIRCLE THE WORD YOU THINK BEST DESCRIBES THE HERO BASED ON HIS OR HER OUTWARD APPEARANCE:

EMBARRASSED
ATTRACTIVE
STUCK UP
DEXTEROUS
INSECURE
EASY

OBNOXIOUS
POWERFUL
FORMIDABLE
CROSS
DISTANT
HOMICIDAL

OUT OF STEP
SECOND RATE
DORKY
SENSIBLE
ENDEARING
APPROACHABLE

SKIN-TO-LYCRA RATIO

Do you feel exploited? Everyone has his or her own comfort level when it comes to costumes, from full body coverage to barely there. If you've been pressured by teammates or a partner into wearing something that you feel is too revealing, it's best to confront the issue now.

C'MON, PRINCESS X'HALA! JUST BECAUSE EVERYONE ON YOUR HOME PLANET **COVERS THEIR VOLUPTUOUS ORANGE BODIES WITH BURLAP** DOESN'T MEAN THAT'S HOW WE DO IT ON EARTH! WON'T YOU AT LEAST TRY ON THE **CREPE PAPER BUSTIER** THAT SKY RANGER AND I HAD MADE FOR YOU?

BUZZ OFF.

THE CODPIECE ISSUE

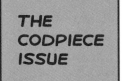

WOMEN AREN'T THE ONLY ONES FACING **UNREASONABLE ANATOMICAL PRESSURES** IN THIS BUSINESS. IT'S A KNOWN, IF UNPUBLICIZED, FACT THAT A FULL 55 PERCENT OF MALE HEROES **STUFF THEIR BIKINI BRIEFS** (AND THAT DOESN'T INCLUDE THE ELASTICALLY POWERED). EVER SINCE A CERTAIN UNNAMED STRONGMAN WAS DISCOVERED TO HAVE **STYROFOAM PECTORALS**, SOME OF THE PRESSURE TO BULK UP HAS EASED, BUT IT REMAINS AN ONGOING CONCERN.

ALTERING COSTUMES

There is a long history of heroes (especially female ones) altering their costumes to fit where they are in their lives, as well as the fashion of the day. Perhaps you've evolved past your costume. Perhaps your costume is an alien organism and must be destroyed before it kills you. Either way, it's a good excuse for a makeover.

SMALL CHANGES CAN MAKE A BIG DIFFERENCE. TRY MODIFYING:

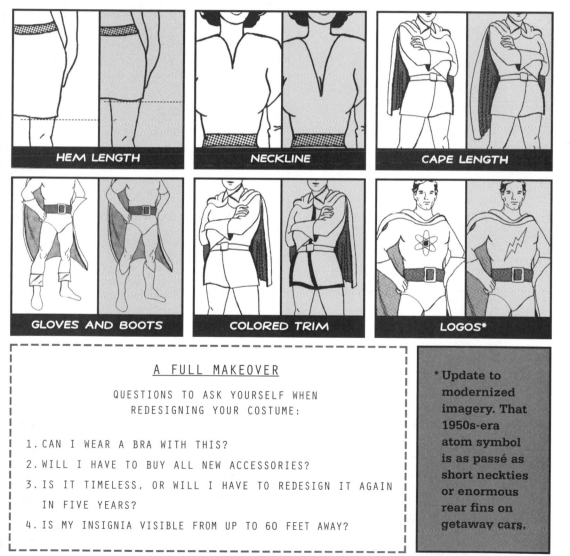

HEM LENGTH

NECKLINE

CAPE LENGTH

GLOVES AND BOOTS

COLORED TRIM

LOGOS*

A FULL MAKEOVER

QUESTIONS TO ASK YOURSELF WHEN
REDESIGNING YOUR COSTUME:

1. CAN I WEAR A BRA WITH THIS?

2. WILL I HAVE TO BUY ALL NEW ACCESSORIES?

3. IS IT TIMELESS, OR WILL I HAVE TO REDESIGN IT AGAIN
   IN FIVE YEARS?

4. IS MY INSIGNIA VISIBLE FROM UP TO 60 FEET AWAY?

* Update to modernized imagery. That 1950s-era atom symbol is as passé as short neckties or enormous rear fins on getaway cars.

SUPER HAIR

Sometimes it may be simpler to cut your hair than design a whole new costume. You'll be amazed at what a difference a new hairstyle can make in how you feel about your appearance. Don't change your hairstyle too frequently, however, or civilians will get the idea that you're constantly holding up traffic at the HQ heliport while you get $200 cuts from celebrity stylists.

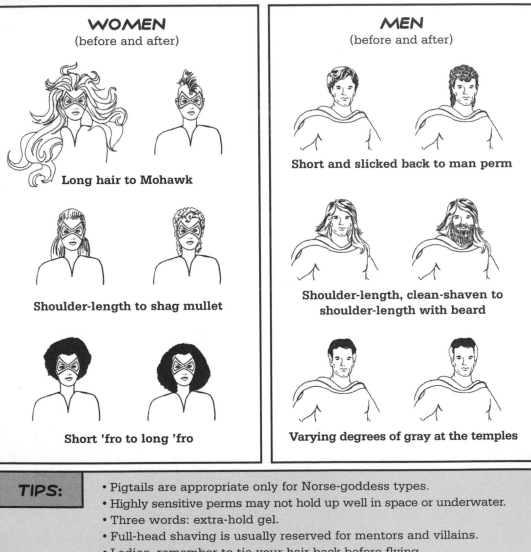

WOMEN
(before and after)

Long hair to Mohawk

Shoulder-length to shag mullet

Short 'fro to long 'fro

MEN
(before and after)

Short and slicked back to man perm

Shoulder-length, clean-shaven to shoulder-length with beard

Varying degrees of gray at the temples

TIPS:
- Pigtails are appropriate only for Norse-goddess types.
- Highly sensitive perms may not hold up well in space or underwater.
- Three words: extra-hold gel.
- Full-head shaving is usually reserved for mentors and villains.
- Ladies, remember to tie your hair back before flying.

BEHIND THE MASK: ARE YOU HIDING FROM YOURSELF?

IF YOU HAVE A SECRET IDENTITY, THEN YOUR SUPERHERO COSTUME MOST LIKELY INCLUDES A MASK. BUT HAVE YOU EVER STOPPED TO THINK ABOUT WHAT MESSAGE YOUR MASK MAY BE SENDING?

FULL COWL

Your identity is completely obscured, and your expressions are entirely unreadable. The public finds you aloof and punctilious. **Some may think you're a sociopath.**

HALF COWL

Your identity is completely obscured, but the public can make out basic expressions such as smiles or frowns. **The public finds you enigmatic, yet obliging.**

EYE MASK*

Your identity is completely obscured, and a wide array of expressions are readable. **The public finds you amiable and benevolent.**

NO MASK

You can hope that a creative costume and hairpiece obscure your secret identity, but without a mask you will most likely be recognizable. Your unmasked visage will allow the public to easily decipher your expressions, and the intrepid citizenry will find you approachable. This is clearly not advised if you are hoping to maintain a secret identity.

* It is a surprising fact that the narrowest eye mask can obscure your true identity from even your closest friends.

PRACTICAL COSTUME CONCERNS

ENSURE THAT YOUR COSTUME INTERACTS WELL WITH YOUR POWERS **(FIRE RETARDANT, ABLE TO ACCOMMODATE SIZE CHANGE, ETC.).** IF YOU THINK THIS MAY BE AN ISSUE FOR YOU, CONSIDER A MATERIAL MADE OUT OF UNSTABLE MOLECULES. IT'S IMPORTANT THAT YOU FEEL COMFORTABLE IN WHATEVER YOU'RE WEARING.

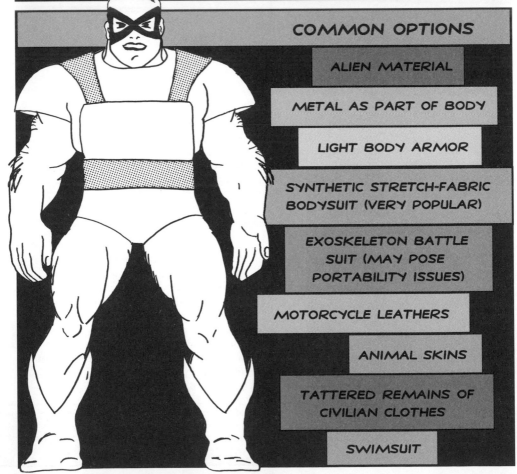

COMMON OPTIONS

ALIEN MATERIAL

METAL AS PART OF BODY

LIGHT BODY ARMOR

SYNTHETIC STRETCH-FABRIC BODYSUIT (VERY POPULAR)

EXOSKELETON BATTLE SUIT (MAY POSE PORTABILITY ISSUES)

MOTORCYCLE LEATHERS

ANIMAL SKINS

TATTERED REMAINS OF CIVILIAN CLOTHES

SWIMSUIT

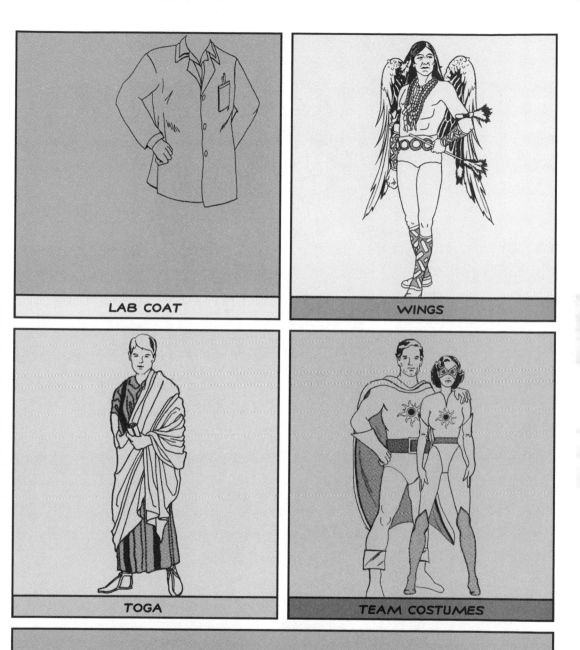

LAB COAT

WINGS

TOGA

TEAM COSTUMES

A note on team costumes: Team costumes, like bridesmaid dresses, may create resentment, as the same costume may look very different in terms of fit and color from one person to the next. Also, while promoting a "team identity," the identical costumes may make some wearers feel as if their self-expression is being compromised. If possible, consider allowing accessories that reflect each team member's personal style.

CHAPTER #13

IT IS TEMPTING TO STEREOTYPE IMMORTALS AS **ALL-SEEING, INSCRUTABLE BEINGS** WITH LONG BEARDS AND THUNDER-BOLTS. AS WITH ALL STEREOTYPES, THIS ONE IS BASED IN SOME FACT, BUT IT IS IMPORTANT TO RECOGNIZE THAT THERE ARE OTHER TYPES OF IMMORTALS AS WELL. THERE ARE THOSE WHO'VE BEEN AROUND FOR THOUSANDS OF YEARS, AND THEN THERE ARE THOSE WHO'VE BEEN AROUND **SINCE BEFORE** THE **BIG BANG**. SOME IMMORTALS ARE THE LAST OF THEIR KIND, AND SOME CAN TAKE THE **RAINBOW BRIDGE** BACK TO THEIR MYTHICAL HOME ANYTIME THEY'RE FEELING LONELY. SOME IMMORTALS LIVE OUT THEIR EXISTENCE IN ONE BODY, AND SOME ARE REINCARNATED EVERY GENERATION OR SO. ALL FACE AN INTERESTING ARRAY OF ISSUES. HERE ARE JUST A FEW.

IMMORTALITY VS. INVULNERABILITY

It's important to keep in mind that there is a distinction between **invulnerability** and **immortality**. Just because bullets, lack of oxygen, or atomic bombs won't do you in, that doesn't mean the passage of time won't do the trick. Also, many heroes with altered metabolisms age at a slower rate than the average citizen. This may be subtle enough that such heroes can deflect questions with explanations involving Grecian Formula, or it may be extreme enough that they face some of the same problems as "real" immortals, defined here as those who simply do not age at all once they reach adulthood. Regardless, it should be noted that the following advice is intended for "real" immortals and should not be applied to so-called slow-agers.

STAY ENGAGED

It can be a challenge to remain integrated with Earth rather than just retreating to live among the gods. Lord knows, Earth can be BORING. But remember, it is your duty to live among mortals and help them combat evil. One fun way to pass the time is to pick a primitive culture and convince them you're some sort of god. That way you can subtly influence their development in positive ways without totally blowing their minds, and assuage your own ego at the same time. This can, however, lead to dangerous levels of narcissism.

PRACTICE NONATTACHMENT

AVOID FALLING IN LOVE.
SERIOUSLY. JUST AVOID IT.

SIGNS YOU MAY BE A NARCISSIST

YOU KEEP CARVING YOUR LOGO INTO THE SIDES OF BUILDINGS OR MOUNTAINS.

YOU RUN FOR OFFICE.

YOU LEAVE YOUR DANGER SIGNAL ON ALL THE TIME.

YOU CAN'T BE BOTHERED TO SAVE GOTHAM BECAUSE YOU'VE GOT TO WORK OUT WITH YOUR PERSONAL TRAINER.

YOU THINK YOU LOOK REALLY GOOD IN SPANDEX.

YOU NAME ALL OF YOUR INVENTIONS AFTER YOURSELF.

YOU ARE CONSTANTLY LECTURING COLLEAGUES ON THE WAY THINGS ARE BASED ON YOUR VAST LIFE EXPERIENCE.

YOU'VE ERECTED MORE THAN THREE STATUES OF YOURSELF.

YOU DRESS YOUR SIDEKICK AND PET IN COSTUMES IDENTICAL TO YOUR OWN.

A note on messianic complexes: Narcissism can be exceedingly dangerous in someone who is very powerful, as it can quickly develop into a messianic complex. If you think you or someone you know may be suffering from a messianic complex, seek professional help immediately. Left untreated, a messianic complex can lead to the end of the world.

CHAPTER #14

PSYCHOLOGICAL ISSUES RELATED TO SPECIFIC POWERS

EVERYONE KNOWS THAT SUPERPOWERS COME WITH BAGGAGE. IT'S **TOUGH ENOUGH BEING A KID** WITHOUT HAVING TO WORRY ABOUT ACCIDENTALLY **SLAYING SOMEONE** WITH A **MENTAL ENERGY BOLT.** YET MOST SUPERHEROES, BY THE TIME THEY REACH ADULTHOOD, FEEL THAT THEY HAVE THEIR POWERS MORE OR LESS UNDER CONTROL. INDEED, THEY CAN'T IMAGINE LIVING **WITHOUT FINS.** SOME SUPERHEROES, HOWEVER, DEVELOP NEUROSES DIRECTLY RELATED TO THE VERY ABILITIES THAT MAKE THEM SPECIAL. AS POWERS ARE SO ENTRENCHED IN THE SUPERHERO PERSONA, THESE **LATENT NEUROSES** CAN BE EXTREMELY TRICKY TO TACKLE.

GUILT AND X-RAY VISION

POSSESSORS OF X-RAY VISION MAY FIND THEMSELVES OCCASIONALLY PARALYZED WITH GUILT. YOU MIGHT WONDER IF YOU ARE **NO BETTER THAN A PEEPING TOM**. WHEN A PASSING GLANCE AT A BUILDING CAN YIELD FAR TOO MUCH INFORMATION ABOUT ITS INHABITANTS, IT'S HARD NOT TO FEEL THAT ONE'S SUPERPOWER IS **A BIT TAWDRY**. KEEP IN MIND THAT WHAT PEOPLE DON'T KNOW WON'T HURT THEM. **JUST DON'T LEER.**

PERSONAL BOUNDARIES AND TELEPATHY

MIND READERS SOMETIMES HAVE TROUBLE ESTABLISHING **PERSONAL BOUNDARIES**. INDEED, THE VERY NOTION IS A FOREIGN CONCEPT. SUFFICE IT TO SAY THAT INCREDIBLE AS IT MAY SEEM, SOME THINGS ARE BEST KEPT TO YOURSELF. REMEMBER, JUST BECAUSE **YOU KNOW WHAT EVERYONE IS THINKING**, THAT DOESN'T MEAN THAT EVERYONE WANTS TO KNOW WHAT **YOU'RE** THINKING.

EGO AND SUPER-STRENGTH

WHEN YOU CAN JUGGLE TRUCKS, IT'S HARD NOT TO FEEL LIKE YOU ARE A **GIFT TO ALL MANKIND.** YET YOU MAY FIND THAT YOUR FRIENDS WILL TIRE OF YOUR **STRONGMAN ANTICS** AND ASK YOU TO PLEASE STOP PICKING THEM UP AND TOSSING THEM IN THE AIR. THEY WILL APPRECIATE ANY MODESTY YOU CAN MUSTER. **EVEN FALSE MODESTY.**

INSECURITY AND INVISIBILITY

HAVING PEOPLE **LOOK THROUGH YOU ALL DAY** CAN TAKE A TOLL ON ONE'S SELF-ESTEEM. ARE YOU THAT **TRANSPARENT?** OF COURSE THE ANSWER IS YES, SO YOU MIGHT WANT TO FIND OTHER WAYS TO **STAND OUT.** CONSIDER WRITING A NOVEL OR DEVELOPING YOUR ABILITIES AS A **CONVERSATIONALIST.**

I'VE BEEN DOING A LITTLE **RESEARCH** ABOUT THE **NIHLISM OF MODERN TECHNOLOGICAL SOCIETY.**

CHAPTER 15

ORIGIN STORIES AND THEIR PSYCHOLOGICAL IMPACTS ON THE NOTION OF SELF

How DID YOU GET YOUR POWERS? **ARE YOU AN ALIEN?** WERE YOU STUNG BY A RADIO-ACTIVE INSECT? **BOMBARDED WITH GAMMA OR OMEGA RAYS?** MANY ONGOING PSYCHOLOGICAL DEFICIENCIES CAN BE TRACED DIRECTLY BACK TO A SUPERHERO'S **ORIGIN STORY.** TAKING OWNERSHIP OF YOUR ORIGIN IS AN IMPORTANT STEP IN YOUR JOURNEY TO **ACCEPTANCE AND CLOSURE.** HERE'S A FUN EXERCISE! LOOK UP YOUR ORIGIN STORY (AND THOSE OF YOUR FRIENDS) AND SEE IF THE NEUROSIS DOESN'T SEEM **A TAD FAMILIAR:**

1. MUTANT

You are shunned by the world at large and vilified by the dominant social order. No one likes you. This can lead to a fear of people or society.

DIAGNOSIS: ANTHROPOPHOBIA.

2. SCIENTIFIC EXPERIMENT

Once you were a great scientist. Now you fear technology. You may also blame yourself for failing to bolt down the neural inhibitor.

DIAGNOSIS: TECHNOPHOBIA.

3. RADIOACTIVE BUG BITE

Your newfound appreciation for the power of insect venom may develop into a violent aversion to spiders.

DIAGNOSIS: ARACHNOPHOBIA.

4. ALIEN

You live among humankind, but you are always alone. You are unhappy, isolated, and depressed.

DIAGNOSIS: ALIENATION.

5. EXPOSURE TO RADIATION

You dread the cancerous effects of your radiation exposure and obsess about infertility and hair loss. Regular checkups with an oncologist may assuage some of your anxiety, but not all of it.

DIAGNOSIS: FEAR OF CANCER.

6. INJECTION WITH EXPERIMENTAL ILLEGAL DRUG

You said you'd do it just once, but it made you feel so powerful . . .

DIAGNOSIS: DRUG ADDICTION.

7. YOU ARE SMART AND RICH

Others think you bought your powers or, worse, that your powers are nothing more than the gadgetry and automotive superiority of the landed gentry. You are dismissed by most heroes as a poseur and were not invited to join the local superhero association.

DIAGNOSIS: SOCIAL ANXIETY.

8. INVENTION (SHRINKING GAS, METAL ARMOR, ETC.)

People are trying to steal your invention. They're always watching you. As soon as you let your guard down, they're going to steal it and then you'll be feeble and powerless.

DIAGNOSIS: PARANOIA.

9. YOU WERE GIVEN YOUR POWERS BY THE GOVERNMENT

The only missions you're sent on involve foreign heads of state and warring armies. You fear villains in uniforms, especially if they have an accent.

DIAGNOSIS: XENOPHOBIA.

10. SORCERY

Your powers are fleeting.
If magic created them, magic can take them away.

DIAGNOSIS: YOU FEAR THINGS YOU DON'T UNDERSTAND.

11. YOU FOUND OR WERE GIVEN A SPECIAL WEAPON OR PIECE OF JEWELRY

You don't deserve your gift. It will just get taken away, or you'll lose it, or you'll accidentally leave it in your pocket and put it through the washing machine. You are unworthy and ill equipped

DIAGNOSIS: MILD SELF-LOATHING.

12. LIGHTNING STRIKE

Your powers are a fluke, and when lightning strikes twice you'll be out of luck.

DIAGNOSIS: FEAR OF STORMS.

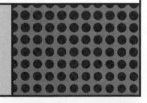

13. YOU'RE PART OF A MYTHICAL RACE

You leave your world/dimension/time to do good works and end up stuck on Earth, helping out a species that can't be bothered to say thank you.

DIAGNOSIS: HOMESICKNESS.

14. YOU'RE A GOD

Well, good for you!

A note on "repressed" origin stories: It is not unusual for a hero to have no memory of his or her origin. But in an age when a "sexy" origin story can redefine a hero's career, there is tremendous pressure to unearth one's beginnings. It is dismaying how many reports have surfaced recently of superheroes "recovering" lost memories that miraculously explain the source of their powers. Be suspicious of such recovered memories, and research these so-called Origin Recovery Clinics carefully before patronizing one.

MAINTAINING A COHERENT NARRATIVE

As you learn more about yourself and where you come from, some aspects of **your origin story** may not jibe with others. For instance, you might think that your parents were gypsies, only to later discover that the gypsies merely adopted you and that **your real mother** was an **alien queen who died in childbirth.** So you ask a few more questions and find out that your mother was **not an alien queen** after all, but actually a **rogue shape-shifter** impersonating an alien queen who did not in fact die, but abandoned **you and your twin brother** because she was afraid of your father, who is, surprise, **a big-shot galactic warlord** and, by total coincidence, your **arch nemesis.** Resolving these sorts of "continuity" issues usually requires sitting down and sorting through your past, teasing out which aspects are true and which can be explained away through poor memory, alternate histories, or other means. Remember, you and only you have the right to tell your own story.

ORIGIN-STORY FAQ

Q: My past is a puzzle wrapped inside an enigma hidden in the belly of a sphinx. How will I ever uncover the truth?

A: A hazy past can be very frustrating. Try sorting through old toys, family photographs, and diaries. Pay special attention to birth certificates, the engravings inside wedding rings, and classified government documents. In a pinch, employ the service of a powerful telepath or private investigator. If you find that you have been brainwashed, you're probably out of luck and should do your best to move on.

CHAPTER #16

Once you've identified **A DENT IN YOUR PSYCHOLOGICAL ARMOR**, YOU MAY DECIDE TO DO SOMETHING ABOUT IT. BUT **GROUP COUNSELING SESSIONS** CAN BE **EMBARRASSING**, AND **BEHAVIORAL MODIFICATION** CAN BE **TIME-CONSUMING AND EXPENSIVE**. FIRST, CONSIDER TAKING MATTERS INTO YOUR OWN HANDS. TO ILLUSTRATE, HERE ARE SOME SIMPLE, PROVEN TECHNIQUES FOR OVERCOMING THE MOST **COMMON SUPERHERO ANXIETIES**.

FEAR OF FLYING

This one is surprisingly common. Hurtling one's body through the air is **no picnic**.

WHAT YOU NEED:

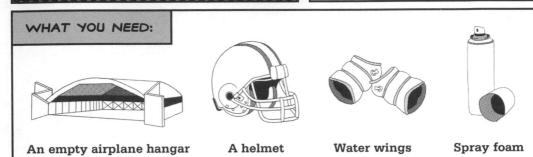

An empty airplane hangar **A helmet** **Water wings** **Spray foam**

Don helmet and water wings. Try flying short distances first. Carry spray foam in case of an emergency landing. Once you've mastered ten yards without feeling queasy, increase your distance incrementally until you can traverse the length of the hangar.

FEAR OF SUFFOCATING IN SPACE

For some reason, civilians on Earth have gotten the idea that **you can't breathe in space.** Of course, that isn't the case. Superheroes zoom about all day and night through the cosmos and do just fine without the hassle of a clunky respirator. Nevertheless, heroes who have internalized the **whole "space is a vacuum" myth** may find that their knees go weak when they're faced with completely run-of-the-mill space work.

WHAT YOU NEED:

Space **A deep-space cruiser** **A clunky respirator**

Blast off into orbit in your nifty deep-space cruiser. Now hold the respirator to your mouth and leave the spacecraft. When comfortable, remove the respirator. Breathe normally. See? You're just fine.

FEAR OF PLANET-SWALLOWING IMMORTAL VILLAINS

WHAT YOU NEED:

A vacation

In the superhero business it is inevitable that you will run into a **planet-swallowing immortal villain**. True, this is a scary notion. But remember: There are lots of planets. Planets get destroyed all the time. Even whole galaxies get destroyed. **The odds of your knowing someone in one of those galaxies are very, very slim**. So why worry?

FEAR OF LOSING YOUR POWERS

This indicates a subconscious fear that **people do not like you for who you are**, but rather for what you can do. Develop an identity beyond your powers. If you do not have a secret identity, create one. Work on bringing **value to your work** that goes beyond your ability to levitate buildings.

WHAT YOU NEED:

A college degree   A boyfriend/girlfriend   A hobby

CHAPTER #17

SPECIAL ISSUES RELATING TO ORPHANS

THE SUPERHERO BUSINESS ATTRACTS A **GREAT NUMBER OF ORPHANS**, ESPECIALLY IN THE SIDEKICK ARENA. EVEN THOSE WHO ARE NOT ORPHANS OFTEN END UP **LOSING THEIR PARENTS TO GALACTIC RADIATION STORMS** OR **GIANT ROBOTS**. SOMETIMES PARENTS SIMPLY **VANISH INTO THIN AIR**. NATURALLY, BEING AN ORPHAN PRESENTS A WHOLE OTHER SUBGROUP OF **PSYCHOLOGICAL ISSUES**.

WHAT IS CODEPENDENCY?

AM I CODEPENDENT?

T F I ASSUME THAT I AM RESPONSIBLE EVERY TIME A VILLAIN ANNIHILATES A CITY OR TOWN.

T F I HAVE DIFFICULTY EXPRESSING EMOTIONS.

T F I WORRY ABOUT HOW MY COLLEAGUES WILL RESPOND TO MY EMOTIONS.

T F I HAVE DIFFICULTY FORMING AND MAINTAINING CLOSE RELATIONSHIPS WITH PETS AND/OR SIDEKICKS.

T F I FEAR BEING REJECTED BY MY NEMESIS.

T F I HAVE AN UNREALISTIC EXPECTATION THAT I MUST KEEP THE WORLD SAFE FROM THE FORCES OF TYRANNY.

T F I HAVE DIFFICULTY MAKING DECISIONS.

T F I PLACE THE NEEDS OF MY COLLEAGUES ABOVE MY OWN.

T F I FEEL THAT MY SUPERPOWER ISN'T GOOD ENOUGH.

T F I HAVE BEEN TOLD THAT I AM LOYAL "TO A FAULT."

T F I LIKE TO HOLD HANDS IN BATTLE.

CHAPTER #18

DEALING WITH PEOPLE WHO THINK YOU'RE "DIFFERENT"

IT'S A SAD FACT OF LIFE THAT PEOPLE HAVE ALWAYS FELT, AND PROBABLY ALWAYS WILL FEEL, SOME UNEASE AROUND THOSE WHO ARE **VISIBLY DIFFERENT** FROM THEMSELVES. AND LET'S FACE IT, WHEN YOU'RE A **SEVEN-FOOT-TALL WALKING HUNK OF ASPHALT**, YOU'RE DIFFERENT. EVEN IF YOU'RE A MILD-MANNERED FIVE-FOOT, FOUR-INCH COMPUTER SUPPORT SPECIALIST, YOU'LL EVENTUALLY SLIP UP AND USE **YOUR FROST BREATH** TO ICE A TOO-WARM BEER AT THE COMPANY PICNIC, AND WHEN THAT HAPPENS, **YEP, YOU'RE DIFFERENT**. THE FIRST AND MOST IMPORTANT STEP IS TO ADMIT TO YOURSELF THAT YOU REALLY **AREN'T LIKE MOST PEOPLE**, AND THAT'S NOT A BAD THING. THE KEY IS TO WALK THE RAZOR'S EDGE BETWEEN SHAME OR RESENTMENT OVER OTHERS' REACTIONS TO YOU AND EGOTISTICAL PRIDE OVER YOUR SUPERIORITY.

LET YOUR FREAK FLAG FLY

If you're unfortunate enough to have been permanently transformed into an especially unusual-looking hero (Sewage Man, Hideoso, or Scarifica), this is an issue you're forced to deal with 24 hours a day. It can be very challenging to both your self-image and your temper to have civilians flee at the very sight of you. Try thinking of your supposed curse as an opportunity, a chance to show others through your actions and demeanor that they really can't judge people by the freakish chemical composition of their skin, the style of their dress, or how many antlers they have poking out of their back.

DISCUSSION QUESTION:

THE SMART CORPORATION INVENTS A SALVE THAT WILL FINALLY HEAL YOUR SOCIALLY ISOLATING OOZING WARTS. BUT THESE WARTS ARE THE SOURCE OF YOUR POWER.

WHAT DO YOU DO?

CHAPTER #19

MANAGING YOUR EMOTIONS

We ALL HAVE TROUBLE **MANAGING OUR FEELINGS** NOW AND AGAIN. BUT IT IS ESPECIALLY IMPORTANT FOR SUPERHEROES TO HAVE A **FIRM GRIP** ON THEIR EMOTIONS. HOW DO YOUR EMOTIONS AFFECT HOW YOU THINK AND ACT? HOW DO YOUR EMOTIONS AFFECT OTHERS? LEARN TO **MASTER YOUR PASSIONS**, BEFORE THEY MASTER YOU.

ANGER MANAGEMENT

MANY SUPERHEROES HAVE REPUTATIONS AS **"HOTHEADS,"*** AND THAT'S NOT SURPRISING, CONSIDERING ALL THAT SUPERHEROES HAVE TO PUT UP WITH. SUPER VILLAINS. ALIENS WIELDING DELTA ELECTRON GUNS THAT SEND YOU INTO ANOTHER DIMENSION FROM WHICH YOU CAN NEVER ESCAPE. IT'S ENOUGH TO GET ANYONE'S DANDER UP. HOWEVER, IT'S IMPORTANT TO KEEP THINGS IN PERSPECTIVE. DO YOU FIND THAT YOUR RAGE IS INTERFERING WITH YOUR ABILITY TO DO YOUR JOB OR MAINTAIN A RELATIONSHIP? **TRY THE FOLLOWING CALMING TECHNIQUES.**

* For some electrically charged superheroes this is literally true. Ironically, these sorts of "hotheads" tend to be very even-tempered because of the ongoing electroshock treatments caused by their powers. However, they do tend to suffer from mild memory loss.

PRACTICE DEEP-BREATHING EXERCISES.

CRUSH SOMETHING INCONSEQUENTIAL.

GO OFF INTO THE WOODS FOR A WHILE.

USE HUMOR TO DEFLECT THE SITUATION.

OFFER TO HELP CITY OR COUNTY OFFICIALS DESTROY CONDEMNED BUILDINGS OR DISPOSE OF RADIOACTIVE WASTE.

FLY THROUGH THE SUN.

PANIC ATTACKS

THE ONLY THING MORE EMBARRASSING THAN PANICKING IN THE FACE OF A SABER-WIELDING SUPER VILLAIN IS PANICKING BACK AT HQ FOR NO REASON AT ALL. PANIC ATTACKS CAN STRIKE AT ANY TIME AND CAUSE A GREAT DEAL OF DISTRESS TO THOSE EXPERIENCING THEM.

AM I HAVING A PANIC ATTACK?

T F   I FEEL LIGHT-HEADED AND I AM NOT UNDER MIND CONTROL.

T F   I FEEL TINGLY AND HAVE NOT BEEN HIT BY A PARESTHESIASLASER.

T F   I FEEL DIZZY AND AM NOT SPINNING THROUGH THE AIR.

T F   I FEEL DISCONNECTED AND HAVE NOT BEEN REMOVED FROM MY BODY.

T F   I AM HAVING CHILLS AND HAVE NOT BEEN HIT BY A RAY OF FROST.

T F   I HAVE TO PEE.

If you think that you are having a panic attack, stop whatever you are doing and retreat to a quiet place until you calm down, unless you are in the middle of stopping a rampaging platoon of robots, in which case, fight the robots, and then go lie down.

RESURRECTION FATIGUE

BACK AGAIN? What do you do when your friends have had the funeral and moved on, just when you show up **back from the dead**? Sure, the first time **it's a miracle**, but come back from the dead again and you'll find that your coworkers may be **more annoyed than awestruck**. Just take things slow, and try not to spook anyone with stories of the thousand years you spent in the future.

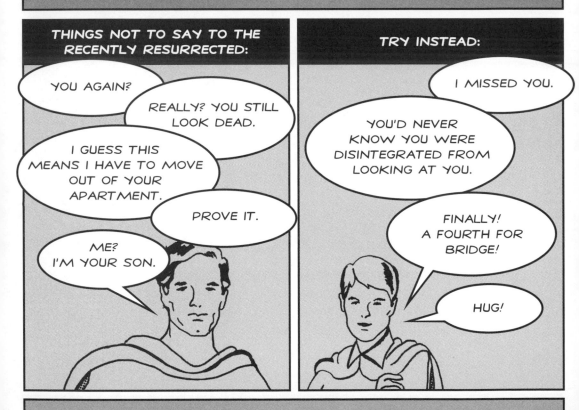

THINGS NOT TO SAY TO THE RECENTLY RESURRECTED:

YOU AGAIN?

REALLY? YOU STILL LOOK DEAD.

I GUESS THIS MEANS I HAVE TO MOVE OUT OF YOUR APARTMENT.

PROVE IT.

ME? I'M YOUR SON.

TRY INSTEAD:

I MISSED YOU.

YOU'D NEVER KNOW YOU WERE DISINTEGRATED FROM LOOKING AT YOU.

FINALLY! A FOURTH FOR BRIDGE!

HUG!

Note: In rare instances, you may be resurrected into a different body from your original one. It could be an enormous mindless beast, an android, a shingle monster, or even a member of the opposite sex. This incredibly complex situation will be the subject of our forthcoming book: *Man, Woman, or Dog: I'm Still Wonderful!* from Omicron Delta Community College Press.

STRESS RELATED TO GALACTIC COURT TRIBUNALS

Appearing before a tribunal of powerful aliens can be **very stressful**. No one likes being the center of **that kind of attention**. And no one likes the idea of being executed. Plus, your friends and family could be called to testify, which would be a drag for them and could breed resentment. Don't let all the hubbub get to you. It's more important than ever that you **remain composed**. Here are some techniques to help.

TALK WITH SOMEONE ABOUT YOUR FEELINGS. (EONS-OLD GALACTIC ELDERS HAVE HEARD IT ALL AND MAKE GOOD LISTENERS.)

DON'T HOLD YOURSELF RESPONSIBLE FOR THAT RACE OF ALIENS YOU ACCIDENTALLY ANNIHILATED. THESE THINGS HAPPEN.

MAINTAIN A NORMAL DAILY ROUTINE AT HQ, BUT LIMIT DEMANDING RESPONSIBILITIES. (LET SOMEONE ELSE ANSWER THE EMERGENCY SIGNAL FOR A CHANGE.)

SPEND TIME WITH FAMILY AND FRIENDS.

TAKE TIME TO CRY.

FOCUS YOUR ENERGY ON LEARNING THE MINUTIAE OF THE KRAZNAR GALAXY'S LEGAL SYSTEM.

CHAPTER #20

MARKETING: EGO BOOSTER OR PSYCHE CRUSHER?

SUPERHEROES LIVE IN THE PUBLIC EYE AND ARE THEREFORE OFTEN **IN THE MEDIA SPOTLIGHT**. THIS CAN BE DIFFICULT FOR THE **SHY**, THE **INSECURE**, AND THE **SOCIALLY AWKWARD**. OBVIOUSLY YOU CAN'T CONTROL WHAT PEOPLE WRITE ABOUT YOU. (EXCEPT IF YOU WORK AS A JOURNALIST IN YOUR SECRET IDENTITY, WHICH IS ONE OF THE REASONS WHY THIS PROFESSION IS SO POPULAR.)

YOU SEND OUT A PRESS RELEASE AND NO ONE RESPONDS.

DO:

Follow up with an e-mail.

Send the release out again to smaller media outlets.

Consider hiring a publicist.

DON'T:

Hurl your local newspaper building into orbit.

DO:

Politely correct your teammate.

Talk to your teammate after the press conference about his/her misconception.

Grin and bear it.

DON'T:

Allow your frustration to activate the recessive DNA that transforms you into a mindless beast whenever you are thwarted.

AT A PRESS CONFERENCE WITH YOUR TEAMMATES, A COLLEAGUE MAKES WHAT YOU BELIEVE TO BE AN INACCURATE STATEMENT ABOUT YOUR ROLE IN AN IMPORTANT BATTLE.

YOUR AGENT CALLS AND TELLS YOU THAT THE **BIG-BUDGET BLOCKBUSTER** ABOUT YOUR LIFE HAS TURNED INTO A **STRAIGHT-TO-VIDEO DISASTER.**

DO:

Review your DVD royalty percentages.

Distance yourself from the final product.

Tell your friends that the movie is stuck in development.

DON'T:

Tell a certain alien warlord that the director is his evil shape-shifter arch nemesis.

DO:

Look at this as an opportunity to work out at the gym and finally have your teeth done.

Pursue televised media opportunities.

Market your own true-to-life lunchboxes.

DON'T:

Pout.
It looks petty.

YOUR **FILM IS A GREAT SUCCESS.** BUT THE ACTOR WHO PLAYS YOU IS MORE ATTRACTIVE THAN YOU ARE, AND YOU LOOK NOTHING LIKE THE "YOU" WHO IS NOW ON **LUNCHBOXES ACROSS THE COUNTRY.** NOW, WHEN YOU SHOW UP AT A BATTLE, CIVILIANS DON'T BELIEVE THAT YOU'RE WHO YOU SAY YOU ARE. EVEN YOUR NEMESES LOOK DISAPPOINTED.

CHAPTER #21

HANGING UP THE CAPE

THOUGH MANY IN THE SUPERHERO COMMUNITY DON'T LIKE TO TALK ABOUT IT, **POWER LOSS** IS MORE COMMON THAN IS GENERALLY ADMITTED. MAYBE YOU'VE BEEN HIT BY THE **DEMUTANTIZING RAY OF DR. NORMALUS** AND INSTANTANEOUSLY REVERTED TO A PLAIN OLD ORDINARY HUMAN. OR MAYBE THE EFFECT IS MORE GRADUAL: AS YOUR BODY SLOWLY **ADJUSTS TO THE ORBIT OF EARTH'S MOON** RATHER THAN SATURN'S, YOU NOTICE THAT LIFTING FIFTEEN TONS IS STARTING TO FEEL MORE **LIKE FIFTY.** IN ANY CASE, THE POTENTIAL FOR PSYCHOLOGICAL DAMAGE IS EXTREME. EVEN NONPOWERED HEROES CAN EXPERIENCE POWERFUL ANGST WHEN A BROKEN BACK, **BANKRUPTCY,** OR A DEGENERATIVE DISORDER CURTAILS THEIR **ACROBATIC DO-GOODING,** OR WHEN THE OMICRON ALIENS FINALLY RETURN AND RETRIEVE THE POWER BOOTS THEY LEFT HERE YEARS AGO. IT'S IMPORTANT TO REMEMBER THAT EVEN WITHOUT POWERS, YOU'RE STILL A **VALUABLE MEMBER OF SOCIETY** AND FULLY CAPABLE OF LEADING A RICH, REWARDING LIFE. OF COURSE, THAT DOESN'T MEAN SOME ADJUSTMENT WON'T BE NECESSARY.

REINVENTING YOUR PERSONAL PARADIGM

Should you lose your powers **or simply grow weary** of the superhero game, any pension you receive may not be enough to grant you the lifestyle to which you've become accustomed. Weekly expeditions to the far corners of the globe are more expensive when you're **flying commercial**, rather than depending on your own hypersonic speed. Even if you're financially secure, few retired superheroes adjust well to a relaxed, **activity-free** lifestyle. Many of the same careers used as secret identity covers are popular among ex-heroes (and are one of the benefits of maintaining a solid civilian career).

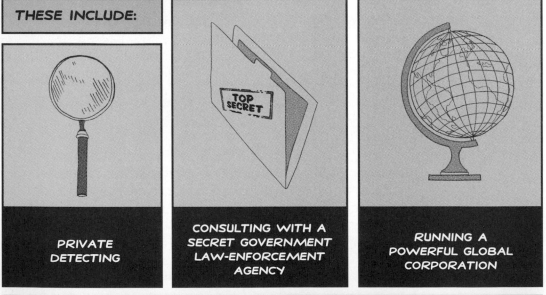

THESE INCLUDE:

PRIVATE DETECTING

CONSULTING WITH A SECRET GOVERNMENT LAW-ENFORCEMENT AGENCY

RUNNING A POWERFUL GLOBAL CORPORATION

These professions allow you to maintain contacts in the superpowered community, which of course will help your own inquiries, and allow you to call on paranormal aid if the going gets sticky.

Another option for those inveterate heroes who **can't shake the cape** is to be a mentor or, if that doesn't work out, adopt the humiliating but proximal position of **gardener**, tech support, or **majordomo** to another hero or group of heroes. That way, if you decide to jump back in, you're right where the action is. If you're quitting the game because of **disillusionment** or a sense of futility, you're better off trying something as far from your former life as possible. One very famous superhero we know was able to anonymously blend into the **lunchroom staff** of Grover Cleveland Middle School.

WHEN TO TAKE TIME OUT FROM ADVENTURING

YOUR GIRLFRIEND HAS EATEN A GALAXY.

YOUR MYTHICAL RACE DISOWNS YOU.

YOU HAVE A BIG HIGH SCHOOL MATH TEST COMING UP.

THE THRILL OF STOPPING METEORS SPEEDING TOWARD EARTH IS NOT WHAT IT USED TO BE.

YOU ARE SWEPT UP IN A TEMPORAL ANOMALY AND SEEMINGLY VANISH FROM EXISTENCE.

YOU WANT TO GET MARRIED AND MOVE TO ALASKA.

YOUR BIOCHEMIST HUSBAND BUILDS A GIANT ROBOT THAT TRIES TO KILL YOU.

NOTHING YOU DO MAKES ANY DIFFERENCE ANYWAY.

HANDWRITING ANALYSIS

EXAMPLES OF HERO HANDWRITING

HARDWORKING

STRAIGHTEN UP AND FLY RIGHT, KIDS!

ARROGANT

Vitamins, Not Violence!

TACKLES PROBLEMS
AT HAND

May Your Sun Always Shine!
Sincerely,
Solaris

PURPOSEFUL AND DISCIPLINED,
GOOD HAIR

EXAMPLES OF SIDEKICK HANDWRITING

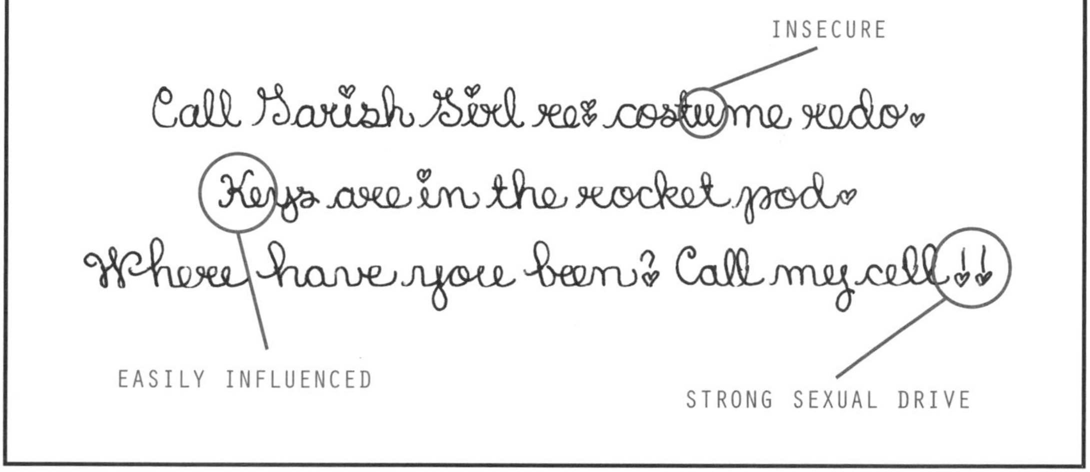

INSECURE

Call Garish Girl re: costume redo

Keys are in the rocket pod

Where have you been? Call my cell !!

EASILY INFLUENCED

STRONG SEXUAL DRIVE

EXAMPLES OF NEMESIS HANDWRITING

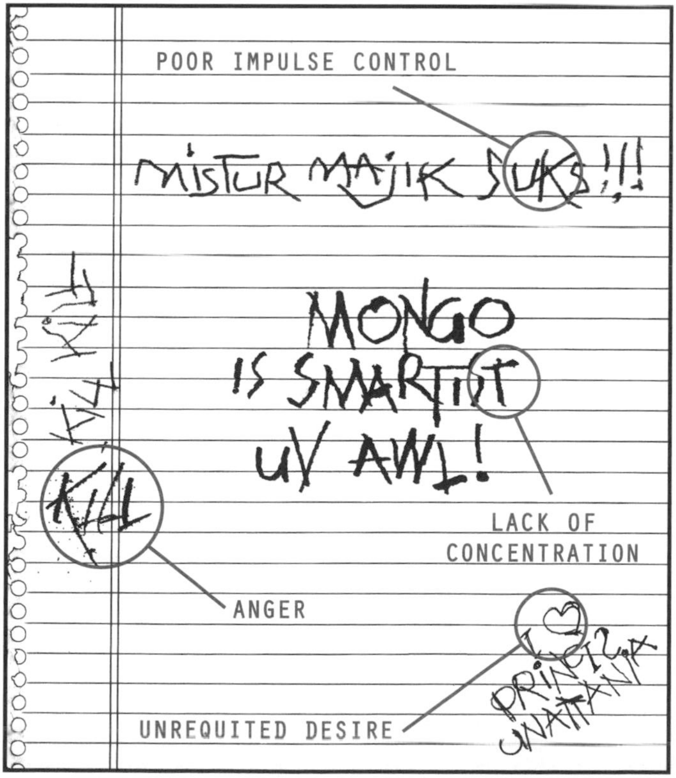

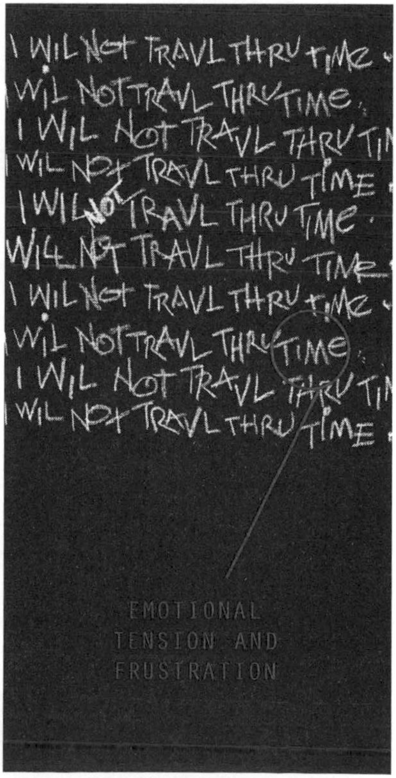

POOR IMPULSE CONTROL

MISTUR MAJIK SUKS !!!

MONGO IS SMARTIST UV AWL!

LACK OF CONCENTRATION

KILL

ANGER

UNREQUITED DESIRE

PRINT2 NATTANI

I WIL NOT TRAVL THRU TIME
WIL NOT TRAVL THRU TIME
I WIL NOT TRAVL THRU TIM
WIL NOT TRAVL THRU TIME
I WIL NOT TRAVL THRU TIME
WIL NOT TRAVL THRU TIME
I WIL NOT TRAVL THRU TIME
WIL NOT TRAVL THRU TIME
I WIL NOT TRAVL THRU TIM
WIL NOT TRAVL THRU TIME

EMOTIONAL
TENSION AND
FRUSTRATION

SELF-HYPNOSIS

RELAX IN COMFORTABLE POSITION.

COUNT BACKWARD FROM 100.

REPEAT:
"I'M GOOD ENOUGH, I'M STRONG ENOUGH,
AND THIS CAPE MAKES ME LOOK GREAT."

ROLE PLAYING

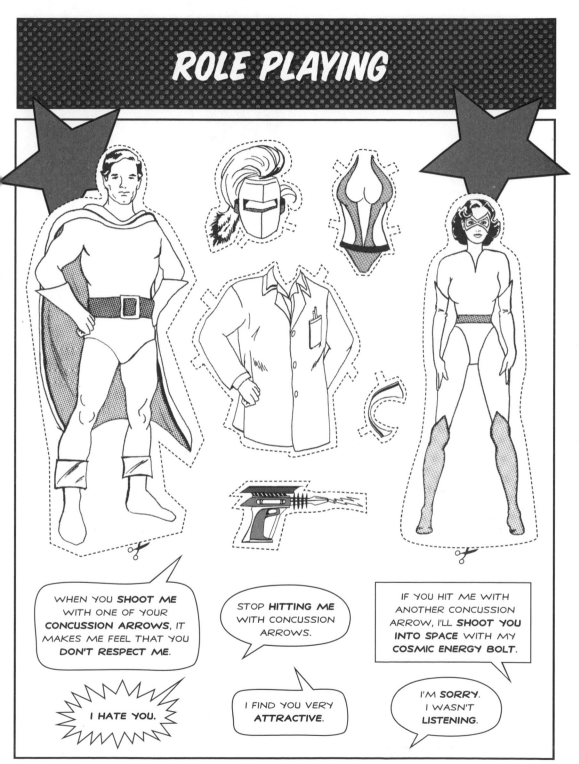

ABOUT THE AUTHORS

Chelsea Cain is the author of several books, including *The Hippie Handbook: How to Tie-Dye a T-shirt, Flash a Peace Sign, and Other Essential Skills for the Carefree Life*. **Marc Mohan** writes about movies for the *Oregonian*. Together, they use their super powers to protect and serve the greater Portland, Oregon, metropolitan area.

ABOUT THE ILLUSTRATOR

Lia Miternique's illustrations have appeared in several books, including *The Hippie Handbook*. She is the owner of Avive Design in Portland, Oregon.